VOLUME 13 • ISSUE 2 • FALL 2021

GREAT COMMISSION
RESEARCH JOURNAL

Published by the Great Commission Research Network

Published by the Great Commission Research Network (GCRN)
GCRN's Registered Agent: Corporation Service Company
7716 Old Canton Road, Suite C
Madison, MS 39110

www.greatcommissionresearch.com

Printed in the United States of America by Martel Press, Claremont, CA

Correspondence: 695 E. Bougainvillea St., Azusa, CA 91702 USA

THE PURPOSE of the *Great Commission Research Journal* is to communicate recent thinking and research related to effective church growth and evangelism.

THE JOURNAL The *Great Commission Research Journal* (formerly, *The Journal of the American Society for Church Growth*) is published semi-annually, Fall and Spring. It is indexed in *Christian Periodical Index* and the *Atla Religion Database*.

ISSN 1947-5837 (print)
ISSN 2638-9983 (online)
ISBN 978-0-9986175-9-6

THE OPINIONS AND CONCLUSIONS published in the Great Commission Research Journal are solely those of the individual authors and do not necessarily represent the position of the Great Commission Research Network.

CONTENTS

GREAT COMMISSION
RESEARCH JOURNAL
2021, Vol. 13(2) 5-20

Innovation in Churches: A Theoretical Framework

David R. Dunaetz, Editor

Abstract

The impact of the COVID-19 pandemic and the many changes in the present socio-cultural context point to the importance of innovation in churches. A theoretical framework for understanding innovation in churches is presented, featuring 6 key elements. These elements include the cultural context of the church and the church's target audience, a culture of innovation within the church, innovations in church programs, processes, and personnel, social capital (social ties) which permits church members to navigate the changes associated with innovation, program loss (that which is lost when programs change), and progress toward the church's goals. The church's goals and the church's context determine which innovations would be most appropriate. A culture of innovation and strong social ties permit innovations to be implemented successfully. Program losses may reflect aspects of the church's goals that are neglected when innovations are implemented.

The COVID-19 pandemic of 2020-2021 has demonstrated how important innovations in churches are. For most churches, especially in the developed world with strict procedures in place to protect public health, virtually all programs and meetings in their existing form stopped due to stay-at-home orders which varied in frequency and duration according to the severity of the pandemic and policies of local, state, and national powerholders. Churches were forced to innovate, as described in some of the articles in this issue of the *Great Commission Research Journal* (e.g., Franks, 2021; Ransom & Moody, 2021). These innovations all represent stories of relative success during trying times. However, not all churches implemented successful innovations and are still trying to recover from the interruptions caused by the pandemic.

To better understand innovation in churches (when it is necessary, what constitutes a successful innovation, what their purpose should be, and what contributes to their success and failure), a model is presented here based on empirical research done both in organizations in general (e.g., Anderson et al., 2014; Gopalakrishnan & Damanpour, 1997; Hurley & Hult, 1998) and in churches specifically (e.g., Covarrubias et al., 2021; Powell & Pepper, 2018). The goal of presenting this model is to help church leaders think clearly about innovation, analyze the role of innovation in their churches, and make changes to more effectively accomplish the Great Commission that Jesus gave us (Matt. 28:18-20).

A Model of Innovation in Churches

A theoretical framework for understanding innovation in churches is presented in the model in Figure 1; the model has six main elements. At the center lies innovation itself, the new ideas, programs, and processes that are introduced into the life of a local church. The principal antecedent to innovation is a culture of innovation within the church, which makes innovation possible. The desired outcome of innovation is progress towards accomplishing the mission of the church. However, if elements of existing programs are lost in the process of innovation, this program loss can reduce, or even erase any progress made toward fulfilling the church's mission. Moreover, the strength of the relationship between innovation and progress is influenced by the social ties linking church members. When church members have strong social ties with each other, innovation is more likely to have a positive effect than when the church members only have weak social ties. All of this lies within a specific cultural context.

This model does not seek to explain all the complexities associated with innovation. Some factors are not included in this model (e.g., the possibility of conflicts escalating and damaging relationships). However, the model seeks to explain how several well-researched phenomena relate to innovation in the context of churches.

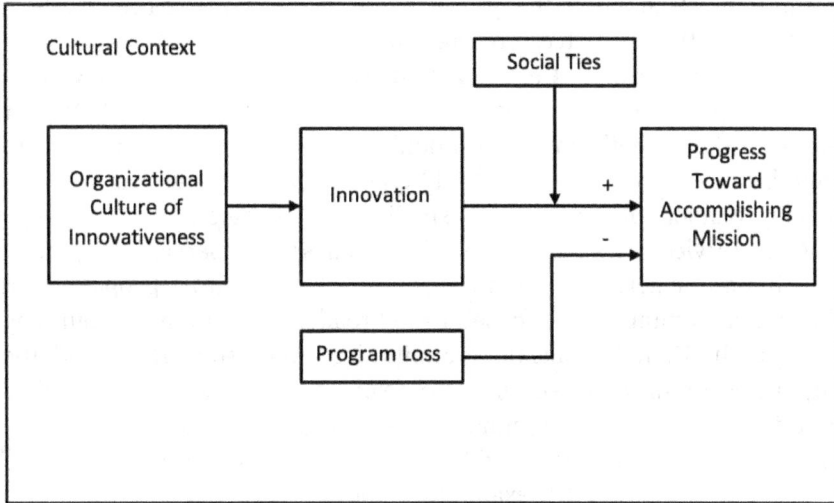

Figure 1. *A Theoretical Model of Innovation in Churches*

Innovation

Church innovation can be defined as the introduction of "new processes, products, or ideas" into the church (Hult et al., 2004, p. 429). In churches, the most visible forms of innovation are new programs and activities but may also include the introduction of new technologies (as was common during the COVID-19 pandemic), new administrative structures (such as adding staff), or new processes (such as determining who will be on a church board and other forms of leadership selection).

Innovation can be conceived as a two-step process, the first stage consisting of the generation of new ideas and the second stage consisting of implementation. The first stage has much overlap with creativity. However, creativity is typically considered an individual activity whereas innovation occurs at the organizational level, or at least at the group level within organizations (Adams et al., 2004). The creation of new ideas may also occur outside the church, but innovation requires adapting the idea to the church's context. The second stage, implementation, consists of making the new program, activity, or process a reality within the organization. The distinction between these stages may be somewhat superficial because the creation and implementation of new processes is not a linear process. As soon as leaders start implementing an idea, they may realize that it needs to be modified, requiring the generation of new ideas; this process may continue back and forth indefinitely.

Church innovation can take many forms. Several dimensions are useful for understanding the types of innovations that have been made in the past and those which can be made now.

Product versus Process Innovations. Product innovations (Fritsch & Meschede, 2001; Gopalakrishnan & Damanpour, 1997) are new products that benefit an organization's clients or service recipients. In churches, these new products would typically be programs (e.g., Awana, Sunday School, or training for small group leaders), activities (e.g., worship services or small group Bible studies), and services (e.g., food distribution or neighborhood tutoring) that benefit either people within the church community or those in the broader community surrounding the church. Digital monastic communities (Anderson, 2021) and the interactive, online children's ministry (Norregaard & Ng, 2021) described in this issue are product innovations. To generate ideas concerning product innovations, it is useful to think of the main programs or area of ministry of the church. For examples, some churches may view their focal ministries as Worship, Teaching, Evangelism, Missions, and Fellowship. The questions "What are new ways we can worship?" or "What are ways we can improve evangelism in the church?" are questions that can lead to product innovations.

Process innovations, on the other hand, are new tools, technologies, or knowledge that help organizations to improve or create new programs, activities, or services. During the pandemic, most innovations in churches were process innovations. Examples include the use of Zoom and Facebook Live for broadcasting worship services or meeting together in small groups (Ransom & Moody, 2021; Sellers, 2021). When the pandemic hit, in order to maintain, or perhaps even improve, existing programs, new processes needed to be introduced (e.g., online broadcasting and online meetings) into churches.

Radical versus Incremental Innovations. Radical innovations are a clear departure from what was done previously whereas incremental innovations improve what is currently being done (Gopalakrishnan & Damanpour, 1997). Most innovations in churches, apart from times of crisis, are incremental with the goal of gradually improving or adjusting a program in light of new insights, new technologies, or cultural changes. Radical innovations in churches are less common; examples might include training individuals in personal evangelism (popular in the 1970s and 1980s), the introduction of a small groups ministry, or the replacement of time-tested hymns with contemporary worship songs in worship. However, all innovations can be placed along a radical-incremental spectrum and what seems radical in one context may be simply incremental in another. In general, any creative idea that is greeted with

"We've never done it that way before" may be considered a radical innovation in its context (Neighbour, 1973). The likelihood of a radical innovation being successfully implemented is lower than that of an incremental innovation. Organizational openness and social ties (described later in this discussion) are especially important factors influencing the successful implementation of all innovations, and especially of radical innovations.

Technical versus Administrative Innovations. When we think of innovations in churches, we usually think of visible changes in programs, activities, and services. These visible innovations are known as technical innovations because they directly affect what the church does to accomplish its mission (Gopalakrishnan & Damanpour, 1997; Jaskyte, 2011). However, innovations may also be invisible, affecting only how employees of the organization relate to each other and to the organization; these can be classified as administrative innovations. Administrative innovations may include hiring staff who do not appear publicly in the church's ministry, changing the church bylaws or organizational structure (who reports to whom), or creating new human resources practices. Innovative human resource practices may include training for staff, employing additional people in decision-making processes, creating awards for specific types of employee behavior, flexible work hours, placing an emphasis on job variety, or providing greater autonomy (Anderson et al., 2014). Any change in leadership behavior that is not directly seen in the programs, activities, or services offered by the church can be viewed as an administrative innovation. To develop administrative innovations, leaders can ask themselves "How can I treat people differently to more effectively carry out the church's mission?"

Progress Toward Mission Accomplishment

The goal of innovation in a church should be to move towards accomplishing the mission that God has given the church. Without a clear understanding of the church's mission, the choice of what innovations to implement will be muddled. Churches often have mission statements (Church Relevance, 2013; Mullane, 2002) which might specifically focus on fulfilling the Great Commission (Matt. 28:18-20) or a broader description of Christian responsibility. Such a statement provides a standard by which programs and methods can be assessed. Because church innovation is typically the introduction of new programs and activities, a church's mission statement also provides a standard by which innovations can be evaluated. Innovations that are likely to contribute to accomplishing the church's mission should be adopted while those that do not contribute to it should not be prioritized.

In practice, the mission statement of the church may simply reflect an idealized view of the church's values and may be used more to project a specific public image (Mullane, 2002; Swales & Rogers, 1995) than to evaluate programs and activities. Other values may play an important role, sometimes a much more important role, in determining the innovations that are adopted. These values may vary in their legitimacy from a biblical point of view. Providing for the needs of the church staff and their families and maintaining the status quo financially (e.g., not offending large donors) may be among the highest priorities in a church and the determining factor concerning some innovations.

On the less honorable end of questionable factors influencing whether an innovation should be adopted in a church are the leaders' ego needs. Although humility is one of the most important virtues in the Bible (e.g., I Pet 5:5-6, James 4:6-10, Mark 10:42-45), churches, especially large churches, like all organizations, tend to attract potential leaders who may be relatively narcissistic, pursuing their own status and recognition (Campbell et al., 2011; Dunaetz, Jung, et al., 2018; Grijalva et al., 2015; Twenge & Campbell, 2009; Zondag, 2004). Such leaders may adopt innovations that will make them look better because they want to appear on the cutting edge, because they feel entitled to the personal benefits that the innovation may bring them, or because there is some other factor associated with the innovation that grants them status in the eyes of others (Grapsas et al., 2020; Kirby, 2021; Puls, 2020a, 2020b). Nevertheless, church leaders need to fight against these human tendencies and do their best to "seek first the Kingdom of God" (Matt. 6:33) when evaluating what innovations to implement.

Cultural Context

This model of church innovation (Figure 1) sets all the specific elements directly associated with innovation within a cultural context. No innovation can be made, nor can its value be determined, apart from its cultural context. The most obvious role of culture in innovation concerns technology. For the last several millennia, humans have regularly made advances in technology, a progress which has especially accelerated during the past century (Ellul, 1954). The technology available within a culture is strongly linked to the technology available for church innovations, ranging from the advances in gothic architecture permitting more light into church buildings during the medieval period to the use of LED lighting for mood enhancement in contemporary times. Sometimes innovation is very closely linked to the latest technology; if the COVID-19 pandemic had started a year earlier, church innovation might have looked quite different since Zoom video conferencing would have been much less available (Bowles, 2021).

But the cultural context is far more than technology; it includes all the beliefs and values that are generally held by a group of people (Hofstede, 1980; Schein, 2004). The impact of any innovation (positive or negative, weak or strong) will depend on the culture of the people impacted by the innovation, both inside and outside of the church. This culture may include the social and political trends as well as the academic and intellectual issues considered important. Church leaders must evaluate a potential innovation in light of the culture of the intended audience as well as the cultural changes that are taking place in this audience. Some of the macro trends occurring in the world are increased individualism as standards of living rise (Santos et al., 2017; Twenge & Campbell, 2018) and increased political polarization as social media provides echo chambers (Colleoni et al., 2014) and opportunities for trench warfare where debaters on each side of a debate refuse to listen to each other (Karlsen et al., 2017), convincing users (or at least themselves) that no reasonable person would hold an opinion different than their own.

Innovations must therefore respond to the real issues that people are dealing with in this new cultural context, issues similar to those faced by previous generations, but in a cultural context where materialism and online communication play a greater role. Such contemporary issues include loneliness, lack of social skills, obesity, more frequent mental disorders, and dealing with conspiracy theories. Innovations that include new programs and activities to respond to these complex issues will make the gospel more credible (Dunaetz, 2016; Pornpitakpan, 2004) and will enable churches to better accomplish their mission.

A Cultural of Innovativeness within in the Church

Organizational culture reflects the beliefs and behaviors that are generally assumed to be appropriate in a specific organization (Schein, 2004). Churches, like all organizations, tend to develop specific ways of doing things that distinguish them from other churches. A culture of innovativeness is one of the most important predictors of innovation in churches; without such a culture, innovation is far less likely (Ruvio et al., 2014; see also Covarrubias et al., 2021, in this issue). A culture of innovation "provides environmental support for the continuous generation of new ideas and products over time" (Ruvio et al., 2014, p. 1004). In a study of 2800 Australian churches, Powell and Pepper (2018) found that a culture of innovativeness is associated with better-appreciated worship services, stronger relationships among members, stronger personal commitment of leaders to innovation, but only very weakly (and negatively) to church size.

Empirical research has discovered various elements of organizational culture which predict innovations (Hult et al., 2004; Hurley & Hult, 1998; Hurley et al., 2005; Ruvio et al., 2014). These include creativity, organizational openness to new ideas, an orientation toward the future, a willingness to take risks, and proactiveness (Ruvio et al., 2014). All of these can be found in churches; the degree to which they are found is likely to predict how innovative a church will be.

Creativity. Whereas innovation is the adaptation and implementation of new ideas, new programs, and new processes in a specific context, creativity is the generation of the ideas which paves the way for adaptation and implementation. Creativity is the initial process, while adaptation and innovation are subsequent processes for introducing new and improved programs, processes, and other activities in a church (Anderson et al., 2014; Ruvio et al., 2014). Creativity can be defined as "the generation of novel and useful ideas" (Anderson et al., 2014, p. 1298). Such ideas may or may not be implemented, but they must be new and useful to be considered creative (Woodman et al., 1993). Unlike other elements of an innovative culture, creativity may occur primarily at an individual level rather than a group level; it is often easier to come up with a novel and useful idea alone than in a group situation. It is essential, however, that church leaders learn of creative ideas in order to evaluate their relevance to their context; these ideas do not need to come from the leaders themselves, nor do they need to come from within their churches. This is one of the main benefits of being a member of a network of churches (e.g., a denomination) or a network of Christian leaders (either a local network or a national association, such as the Great Commission Research Network). Similarly, reading contemporary ministry-focused literature can be an important source of innovative ideas.

Organizational Openness. It is not enough for leaders simply to be exposed to new, creative ideas to implement innovations. The organization, including the various people in leadership and other stakeholders, needs to be open to new ideas, responding to them with flexibility, and the ability to adapt them to the current situation (de Dreu & West, 2001; Hurley & Hult, 1998; Ruvio et al., 2014). In churches, this means that leaders need to learn about the needs and experiences of their target audience, not just in broad theological terms, but in their specific cultural context to offer innovative programs and activities that can respond to these needs. It also means that there must be a willingness to let go of what has worked in the past but is no longer bringing the church closer to accomplishing its mission. Leaders must be receptive to new ideas, open to other points of view, tolerant of ambiguity and uncertainty, and evaluate ideas using context-specific principles, while remaining faithful to biblical principles which do not vary according to context. When leaders are chosen and as they are developed, openness to new ideas is essential for being able to move from the creativity stage to the implementation stage of innovation.

Future Orientation. Churches that can focus on their future course of actions rather than the past are more likely to be innovative than churches that continually refer to what has worked in the past (Hult et al., 2004; Ruvio et al., 2014). If leaders can foresee what is likely to happen in the church and the culture in general, they will be better able to implement the innovations necessary to best achieve the church's mission. For example, if the church believes that it will become increasingly difficult for individuals to make a stand for Christ and defend what they believe because of the increasing role of social media (Dunaetz, 2019), programs and activities can be developed to respond to the developing needs. A large part of having a successful future orientation is goal setting (Dunaetz, 2013; Latham & Locke, 1991; Locke et al., 1984; Locke & Latham, 1990). Fixing goals for carrying out specific tasks by a specific time usually generates better results than simply attempting to do one's best. Goals need to be revised regularly and to be set for things that leaders can control (e.g., providing 10 teaching sessions per year on why some aspect of Christianity is credible) than things that they cannot control (e.g., 50 conversions per year).

Risk Taking. Once a church experiences a period of success, it can become quite threatening to start instituting changes, even if what has worked in the past is no longer producing the fruit that it once did. However, the more a church is willing to commit resources to programs and personnel when the outcome is not sure, the more likely the church is to be innovative (Hult et al., 2004; Miller & Friesen, 1978; Ruvio et al., 2014). The main problem with risk-taking is that it often results in failure. Clear thinking, wisdom, and gathering all the information one can beforehand may reduce the risk of failure, but it cannot eliminate it if the outcome is genuinely not known. After a failure, it is important to honestly evaluate the outcome (e.g., start by admitting that a new program did not achieve its purposes), learn from the experience, reevaluate if there are any benefits that justify continuing in the same direction, and undo or adapt the changes made if appropriate.

Proactiveness. Churches that are proactive, those which actively search for and plan activities to minister to new audiences, are more likely to be innovative than churches that focus more on problem-solving. The present problems of a church can easily expand to use all the leaders' time and resources. However, proactive leaders will not let present problems monopolize their time but will continue to work on new projects and touch new people. Proactiveness is fundamental to being a missional church (Guder, 1998; Stetzer, 2006; Van Gelder & Zscheile, 2011). However, proactive ministry needs to be focused on accomplishing the mission of the church. It is not rare for a church to emphasize missional activities where the goal is outreach, that is, developing relationships with non-Christians outside the church. However, outreach without evangelism and disciple-making cannot be considered successful. It may even be a sign of an unhealthy church (Dunaetz & Priddy, 2014).

Social Ties

Recent research on innovation in organizations has focused on the important role that social ties and social capital play (Hasan et al., 2020; Kim & Shim, 2018; Zheng, 2010). When there are strong relationships between people within an organization, and even between people in different organizations, innovation is much more likely to be successful. Social capital can be defined as "the sum of the actual and potential resources embedded within, available through, and derived from the network of relations possessed by an individual or a social unit" (Nahapiet & Ghoshal, 1998, p. 243), or more generally as "social networks and the norms of reciprocity and trustworthiness that arise from them" (Putnam, 2000, p. 19).

There are several reasons that social ties and capital are so important for innovation, especially in churches. Whenever an innovation is introduced in a church, there are costs involved. For example, people might regret the loss of a former program, or some new activity might make them feel ill at ease. These potential costs reduce people's willingness to participate in the innovation and may even encourage them to leave the church. However, when a person has strong relationships with others in the church, the costs are reduced (Powell & Pepper, 2018). For example, people who are close to others have access to more information than people who have few connections with others; this information can help them better understand the value of the change and how to navigate it. Moreover, people value high-quality relationships and do not want to lose them, so they will be more willing to stay in the church when changes become difficult. Close relationships with others also permit church members to directly observe how others navigate the changes, providing them with a model that they can follow (Bandura, 1977; Frayne & Latham, 1987). These examples all demonstrate the importance of social capital in a typical church member's response to innovation. But the leader's social capital maybe even more important.

It has already been noted that a pastor's social connections (e.g., within a denomination) may be an important source of creative ideas. But close relationships with other church leaders also permit the pastor to discuss, better understand, and refine an idea before introducing it to the church, making it more likely to produce the desired results. Pastors without such social capital (e.g., pastors who only come across new ideas through what they read) are handicapped because they are more limited in how they can discuss the ideas with other church leaders (Kim & Shim, 2018; Zheng, 2010). Moreover, introducing innovation into a church can be threatening to individuals who benefit from maintaining the status quo. The strength of relationships that church leaders have with others in the church will help them survive the opposition which may occur, which often includes very painful insinuations and false accusations (Rucker & Petty, 2003; Tanner et al., 2012).

In this model of church innovation (Figure 1), an arrow points from social capital to the arrow going from "Innovation" to "Progress toward Accomplishing Mission." This means that social capital moderates (changes) the relationship between the introduction of innovations and accomplishing the church's mission. By itself, social capital does not contribute to innovation or toward accomplishing the church's mission; rather, it strengthens the relationship between innovation and mission accomplishment. It can be viewed as a water spigot; when social capital is high, the spigot is open, and innovations can have a very positive effect. When social capital is low, the spigot is closed or nearly closed, limiting the positive effect that an innovation can produce. For leaders, this means that the ability to lead is influenced by the quality of the relationship between the follower and the leader.

In this issue of the *Great Commission Research Journal*, we present several innovations that churches implemented during the COVID-19 pandemic. Surprisingly, all of the submissions came from small churches with under 250 people. However, this is in line with Powell and Pepper's (2019) study of 2800 Australian churches which found that church size was slightly (but significantly) negatively related to church innovativeness; larger churches had lower innovativeness than smaller churches. Although large churches have far more resources to experiment with new ideas and technologies, the social connections between members (Powell and Pepper, 2019) are much lower in large churches than in small churches. In large churches, overall levels of commitment may be lower (Dunaetz, Cullum, et al., 2018; von der Ruhr & Daniels, 2012) and attenders may decide to stop coming more easily since they have fewer and weaker social connections to keep them in the church and to help them navigate the innovations that are introduced.

Program Loss

The final element in this model of church innovation (Figure 1) is program loss, the elements of a church's program that contribute to accomplishing its mission but which are lost when new programs and other innovations are introduced. Although church leaders do not like to think that their innovations cause losses, humility requires admitting that this may be the case. Examples include changes in depth of biblical exposition that occurred when small group Bible studies replaced Sunday evening services (Rynsburger & Lamport, 2008; Wuthnow, 1994) and the shift in theological emphases when contemporary worship songs replaced historic hymns (Livengood & Ledoux Book, 2004; Ruth, 2015). Whenever innovations are introduced, wise leaders will listen to people's concerns and consider the potential losses that they might incur; sometimes listening and understanding are all that is necessary to help an innovation gain acceptance, especially when relationships are solid.

Conclusion

The model of church innovation in this paper (Figure 1) presents a theoretical framework for thinking about innovation in churches. Innovation is far more complex than responding to crises that occur outside of the church, such as the COVID-19 pandemic. Church leaders need to have a clear understanding of the mission that they are trying to accomplish in the church. They must also be constantly learning about the evolving cultural environment that influences church members continually. Church leaders should develop a culture of innovation in a church which will make the generation and implementation of new ideas more likely. Leaders must also consider the cost of implementing innovation. An especially important factor is the social capital of church members which will enable them to navigate and endure the hardships that innovation might bring.

Although innovation can be complex and risky, the needs of a world without Christ demand that we continue to seek out new ways to fulfill Jesus' Great Commission and help people discover how they can know and follow him.

David R. Dunaetz, General Editor

References

Adams, G., Anderson, S. L., & Adonu, J. K. (2004). The cultural grounding of closeness and intimacy. In D. J. Mashek & A. Aron (Eds.), *The handbook of closeness and intimacy* (pp. 321-339). Erlbaum.

Anderson, D. (2021). Digital monastic communities at Sumter Chapel, Americus, Georgia. *Great Commission Research Journal, 13*(2), 85-88.

Anderson, N., Potočnik, K., & Zhou, J. (2014). Innovation and creativity in organizations: A state-of-the-science review, prospective commentary, and guiding framework. *Journal of Management, 40*(5), 1297-1333.

Bandura, A. (1977). *Social learning theory*. Prentice Hall

Bowles, J. (2021). How Zoom defied its critics and became the go-to video conferencing app for surviving the pandemic. https://diginomica.com/how-zoom-defied-its-critics-and-became-go-video-conferencing-app-surviving-pandemic

Campbell, W. K., Hoffman, B. J., Campbell, S. M., & Marchisio, G. (2011). Narcissism in organizational contexts. *Human Resource Management Review, 21*(4), 268-284.

Church Relevance. (2013). 50 examples of church mission statements. https://www.churchrelevance.com/2013/03/28/50-examples-of-church-mission-statements/

Colleoni, E., Rozza, A., & Arvidsson, A. (2014). Echo chamber or public sphere? Predicting political orientation and measuring political homophily in Twitter using big data. *Journal of Communication, 64*(2), 317-332.

Covarrubias, A., Dunaetz, D. R., & Dykes, W. (2021). Innovativeness and church commitment: What innovations were most important during the pandemic? *Great Commission Research Journal, 13*(2), 49-70.

de Dreu, C. K. W., & West, M. A. (2001). Minority dissent and team innovation: The importance of participation in decision making. *Journal of Applied Psychology, 86*(6), 1191-1201.

Dunaetz, D. R. (2013). Goals and accountability for ministry effectiveness: Insights from psychological science. *Dharma Deepika: A South Asian Journal of Missiological Research, 17*(1), 66-79.

Dunaetz, D. R. (2016). Missio-logoi and faith: Factors that influence attitude certainty. *Missiology: An International Review, 44*(1), 66-77.

Dunaetz, D. R. (2019). Evangelism, social media, and the mum effect. *Evangelical Review of Theology, 43*(2), 138-151.

Dunaetz, D. R., Cullum, M., & Barron, E. (2018). Church size, pastoral humility, and member characteristics as predictors of church commitment. *Theology of Leadership Journal, 1*(2), 125-138.

Dunaetz, D. R., Jung, H. L., & Lambert, S. S. (2018). Do larger churches tolerate pastoral narcissism more than smaller churches? *Great Commission Research Journal, 10*(1), 69-89.

Dunaetz, D. R., & Priddy, K. E. (2014). Pastoral attitudes that predict numerical Church Growth. *Great Commission Research Journal, 5*, 241-256.

Ellul, J. (1954). *La technique ou l'enjeu du siècle*. A. Colin.

Franks, J. (2021). The Quarantine Olympics of Cultivate Church in Athens, Alabama. *Great Commission Research Journal, 13*(2), 73-76.

Frayne, C. A., & Latham, G. P. (1987). Application of social learning theory to employee self-management of attendance. *Journal of Applied Psychology, 72*(3), 387-392.

Fritsch, M., & Meschede, M. (2001). Product innovation, process innovation, and size. *Review of Industrial Organization, 19*(3), 335-350.

Gopalakrishnan, S., & Damanpour, F. (1997). A review of innovation research in economics, sociology and technology management. *Omega, 25*(1), 15-28.

Grapsas, S., Brummelman, E., Back, M. D., & Denissen, J. J. A. (2020). The "why" and "how" of narcissism: A process model of narcissistic status pursuit. *Perspectives on Psychological Science, 15*(1), 150-172.

Grijalva, E., Harms, P. D., Newman, D. A., Gaddis, B. H., & Fraley, R. C. (2015). Narcissism and leadership: A meta-analytic review of linear and nonlinear relationships. *Personnel Psychology, 68*(1), 1-47.

Guder, D. L. (Ed.). (1998). *Missional church: A vision for the sending of the church in North America*. William B. Eerdmans Publishing.

Hasan, I., Hoi, C.-K. S., Wu, Q., & Zhang, H. (2020). Is social capital associated with corporate innovation? Evidence from publicly listed firms in the US. *Journal of Corporate Finance, 62*, 101623.

Hofstede, G. (1980). *Culture's consequences: National differences in thinking and organizing*. Sage.

Hult, G. T. M., Hurley, R. F., & Knight, G. A. (2004). Innovativeness: Its antecedents and impact on business performance. *Industrial Marketing Management, 33*(5), 429-438.

Hurley, R. F., & Hult, G. T. M. (1998). Innovation, market orientation, and organizational learning: An integration and empirical examination. *Journal of Marketing, 62*(3), 42-54.

Hurley, R. F., Hult, G. T. M., & Knight, G. A. (2005). Innovativeness and capacity to innovate in a complexity of firm-level relationships: A response to Woodside (2004). *Industrial Marketing Management, 34*(3), 281-283.

Jaskyte, K. (2011). Predictors of administrative and technological innovations in nonprofit organizations. *Public Administration Review, 71*(1), 77-86.

Karlsen, R., Steen-Johnsen, K., Wollebæk, D., & Enjolras, B. (2017). Echo chamber and trench warfare dynamics in online debates. *European Journal of Communication, 32*(3), 257-273.

Kim, N., & Shim, C. (2018). Social capital, knowledge sharing and innovation of small-and medium-sized enterprises in a tourism cluster. *International Journal of Contemporary Hospitality Management, 30*(6), 2417-2437.

Kirby, B. (2021). *PreachersNSneakers: Authenticity in an age of for-profit faith and (wannabe) celebrities*. Thomas Nelson.

Latham, G. P., & Locke, E. A. (1991). Self-regulation through goal setting. *Organizational Behavior and Human Decision Processes, 50*(2), 212–247.

Livengood, M., & Ledoux Book, C. (2004). Watering down Christianity? An examination of the use of theological words in Christian music. *Journal of Media and Religion, 3*(2), 119-129.

Locke, E. A., Frederick, E., Buckner, E., & Bobko, P. (1984). Effect of previously assigned goals on self-set goals and performance. *Journal of Applied Psychology, 69*(4), 694-699.

Locke, E. A., & Latham, G. P. (1990). *A theory of goal setting and task performance.* Prentice Hall.

Miller, D., & Friesen, P. H. (1978). Archetypes of strategy formulation. *Management Science, 24*(9), 921-933.

Mullane, J. V. (2002). The mission statement is a strategic tool: When used properly. *Management Decision, 40*(5), 448-455.

Nahapiet, J., & Ghoshal, S. (1998). Social capital, intellectual capital, and the organizational advantage. *Academy of Management Review, 23*(2), 242-266.

Neighbour, R. W. (1973). *The seven last words of the church: Or "We never tried it that way before".* Zondervan Publishing House.

Norregaard, E., & Ng, P. (2021). Making online children's ministry interactive in Wheaton, Illinois. *Great Commission Research Journal, 13*(2), 89-93.

Pornpitakpan, C. (2004). The persuasiveness of source credibility: A critical review of five decades' evidence. *Journal of Applied Social Psychology, 34*(2), 243-281.

Powell, R., & Pepper, M. (2018). Local churches and innovativeness: An empirical study of 2800 Australian churches. *Research in the Social Scientific Study of Religion, 29*, 278-301.

Puls, D. (2020a). *Let us prey.* Cascade Books.

Puls, D. (2020b). Narcissistic pastors and the making of narcissistic churches. *Great Commission Research Journal, 12*(1), 67-92.

Putnam, R. D. (2000). *Bowling alone: The collapse and revival of American community.* Simon and Schuster.

Ransom, B., & Moody, B. (2021). Quick responses to community needs in two churches during the pandemic. *Great Commission Research Journal, 13*(2), 95-98.

Rucker, D. D., & Petty, R. E. (2003). Effects of accusations on the accuser: The moderating role of accuser culpability. *Personality and Social Psychology Bulletin, 29*(10), 1259-1271.

Ruth, L. (2015). Some similarities and differences between historic evangelical hymns and contemporary worship songs.". *Artistic Theologian, 3*, 68-86.

Ruvio, A. A., Shoham, A., Vigoda-Gadot, E., & Schwabsky, N. (2014). Organizational innovativeness: Construct development and cross-cultural validation. *Journal of Product Innovation Management, 31*(5), 1004-1022.

Rynsburger, M., & Lamport, M. a. (2008). All the rage: How small groups are really educating Christian adults part 1: Assessing small group ministry practice: A review of the literature. *Christian Education Journal, 5*(1), 116-137.

Santos, H. C., Varnum, M. E. W., & Grossmann, I. (2017). Global increases in individualism. *Psychological Science, 28*(9), 1228-1239.

Schein, E. H. (2004). *Organizational culture and leadership* (3rd ed.). Jossey-Bass

Sellers, K. (2021). Storytelling the Gospel in Hungary: Zooming in on an ancient mode of communication. *Great Commission Research Journal, 13*(2), 77-84.

Stetzer, E. (2006). *Planting missional churches*. Broadmand & Holman.

Swales, J. M., & Rogers, P. S. (1995). Discourse and the projection of corporate culture: The mission statement. *Discourse & Society, 6*(2), 223-242.

Tanner, M. N., Zvonkovic, A. M., & Adams, C. (2012). Forced termination of American clergy: Its effects and connection to negative well-being. *Review of Religious Research, 54*(1), 1-17.

Twenge, J. M., & Campbell, W. K. (2009). *The narcissism epidemic: Living in the age of entitlement*. Simon and Schuster.

Twenge, J. M., & Campbell, W. K. (2018). Cultural individualism is linked to later onset of adult-role responsibilities across time and regions. *Journal of Cross-Cultural Psychology, 49*(4), 673-682.

Van Gelder, C., & Zscheile, D. J. (2011). *The missional church in perspective: Mapping trends and shaping the conversation*. Baker Academic.

von der Ruhr, M., & Daniels, J. P. (2012). Examining megachurch growth: Free riding, fit, and faith. *International Journal of Social Economics, 39*(5), 357-372.

Woodman, R. W., Sawyer, J. E., & Griffin, R. W. (1993). Toward a theory of organizational creativity. *Academy of Management Review, 18*(2), 293-321.

Wuthnow, R. (1994). *Sharing the journey: Support groups and America's new quest for community*. Simon and Schuster.

Zheng, W. (2010). A social capital perspective of innovation from individuals to nations: Where is empirical literature directing us? *International Journal of Management Reviews, 12*(2), 151-183.

Zondag, H. J. (2004). Just like other people: Narcissism among pastors. *Pastoral Psychology, 52*(5), 423-437

GREAT COMMISSION
RESEARCH JOURNAL
2021, Vol. 13(2) 21-36

Identifying Current Gaps in Church Planting Movements Research: Integrating First- and Second-Order Perspectives

Warrick Farah
One Collective

Abstract

The proliferation of church planting movements in least-reached peoples today provides an opportunity ripe for missiological research. Using the online application form for the Movements Research Symposium 2020 of the Motus Dei Network, this article identifies six gaps of understanding in the missiological discourse on movements: 1) Deepening Theological-Missiological Descriptions of Movements, 2) Identifying Best Practices and Effective Movement Strategies, 3) Clarifying Issues of Ecclesiology – Practical, Theological, and Spiritual, 4) Training Movement Catalysts and Practitioners, 5) Highlighting Contextual, Sociological, and Holistic Features of Movements, and 6) Documenting Movements with Respect to Verification, Metrics, and Administration. However, issues of positionality make investigating these gaps difficult, especially considering the problematic insider/outsider dichotomy in research. Opportunities for integration of perspectives are suggested in a way that values a multi-perspectival framework while prioritizing and empowering local research initiatives.

The opportunity for research on church planting movements is unparalleled in Church history due in part to the convergence of three current phenomena: 1) the exponentially growing number of believers coming to faith in movements among least-reached peoples today, up sharply even since 2005 (Long, 2020), 2) the great number of missionaries from both the Global North and South who have exposure to missiological research (Bevans et al., 2015), and 3) the technological ease for virtual network creation and collaboration. For a greater understanding of how we can achieve the biblical "no place left" aspiration for the gospel (Rom. 15:23), we are wise to seize this opportunity for quality research of church multiplication movements among least-reached peoples and nations today.

However, the very idea of *research* is fraught with complex issues, especially considering the relative novelty of the contemporary strategies and phenomena found in today's church planting movements (CPMs) or disciple making movements (DMMs). A CPM is a "rapid multiplication of indigenous churches planting churches that sweeps through a people group or population segment" (Garrison, 2004, p. 21). DMMs, a specific strategy for a CPM, are "lay-led, small-group discipling movements" where the small groups themselves have multiplied (at least up to four generations) and often along social networks. With or without favorable socio-political factors, the engine driving the CPM process tends to be easily reproducible churches with communal, interactive Bible study as their main liturgy (Farah, 2020, p. 3).

With this definition in mind, who sets the agenda for research concerning CPMs? What are the power dynamics involved? Who wants to know what, and for what purpose? Should the agenda be set only by movement catalysts? Or should academics studying World Christianity (i.e. Pachuau, 2018) lead the overall research discourse? What is the value of examining relationships between the academy, mission agencies, movement practitioners, and members of movements themselves? How can traditional denominations, which are increasingly engaging with the subject of movements, learn from this conversation as well?

This article uses data compiled from the application forms for the Motus Dei Network's virtual Movements Research Symposium of October 2020 to identify and analyze potential research themes concerning CPMs. The Motus Dei Network (http://MotusDei.Network) exists for the missiological study of global movements to Christ and is a collaboration between mission agencies, movement practitioners, and academic research centers. On the application for the Symposium, participants were asked to state their opinions as to the most pressing needs for research and inquiry into movements. As we discuss the proposed themes of research that emerged from the responses, we will reflect on the nature of the discussion. What role do emic (insider) and etic (outsider) perspectives play in framing research initiatives focusing on CPMs? These issues are complicated by rarely-reflected-on philosophical issues of positionality and epistemology. As we will see, members of the Global Church can collaborate effectively by appreciating the contributions, perspectives, and methods of one another (1 Cor. 12:25-26).

Identifying Gaps in Movements Research

In the online application to attend the Movements Research Symposium, which was online from July 2019 – September 2020, 126 applicants responded to the question, "*In your opinion, what are the most important aspects of discipleship movements (or church planting movements) that need further research and inquiry?*" While most applicants were men from the Global North, only 15% were from the Global South and 13% of the applicants were women (a few were African and Asian Women). Moving forward, our movements research initiative needs improvement in integrating non-Western and female voices into the conversation. At the same time, the leadership of the Motus Dei Network was encouraged that dozens of agencies and institutions serving in Africa, Asia, and diaspora settings in the Global North were represented in this initial survey. Applicants included indigenous movement catalysts, movement practitioners, researchers, missionaries, and leaders of mission organizations, many with advanced degrees in missiology. The length of answers ranged from two words, for example, "*social forces,*" to 515 words. The length of the median answer was 24 words. Interestingly, differences in suggestions for topics were not discernable when sorting between gender, ethnicity, and regional area of service. Additionally, non-Western catalysts who responded also had answers spread across the various themes (Table 1).

Theme of Suggestion	Number	Percentage
More Robust Biblical Theology and Missiological Description of Movements	21	10.4%
Best Practices and Identifying Strategies for Catalyzing Movements	19	9.5%
Theology of Church and Forms of Churches in Movements	18	9.0%
Training and Maturing Movement Catalysts (Including Theological Training)	18	9.0%
Social Dynamics and Sociological Features of Movements	17	8.5%
Contextualization (Including Arts/Music) and Socioreligious Identity Issues	14	7.0%
Theological and Spiritual Maturity/Health of Disciples and Churches	12	6.0%
Identifying Models of Training for Movement Practitioners	9	4.5%
Impact of Movements on Holistic Community Transformation	9	4.5%
Differing Features of Movements According to Regional Areas/Context	9	4.5%
Sustainability of Movements	9	4.5%
Relationship to the Global Church, Traditional Churches, and Institutions	9	4.5%
Role of Expatriate or Near-Culture Missionary Coaches	8	4.0%
Metrics, Verification, Evaluation, and Reporting	8	4.0%
Issues Related to (the Difficulty of) Starting Movements in the Global North	7	3.5%
Finances/Outside Support of Movements	6	3.0%
Movements in Cities and Urban Contexts	3	1.5%
Movements Starting Movements	2	1.0%
Role of the Supernatural	2	1.0%
Role of Women in Movements	1	0.5%
Total Suggestions	*201*	*100%*

Table 1. *Suggestions for Research about Movements*

To analyze the responses, I used a combination of qualitative content analysis and inductive coding (Schreier, 2012, p. 44). This iterative process allowed for themes and categories to emerge from the data itself (Wildemuth & Zhang, 2009, p. 310). On average, each applicant mentioned 1.6 ideas of research for a total of 201 suggestions grouped into 20 specific categories. For example, one short answer was, *"Biblical foundations, contextualization."* I coded this response as two suggestions: one as the "More Robust Biblical Theology and Missiological Description of Movements" category and the other as "Contextualization (Including Arts/Music) and Socioreligious Identity Issues," respectively.

Responses were diverse and numerous with, interestingly, no overwhelming consensus. I will combine and reflect on some of the significant suggestions and salient responses in the sections that follow. From these 20 categories of suggestions from those who applied to the Movements Research Symposium, six themes emerged representing gaps or unknown areas in missiological research on church planting movements.

1. Deepening Theological-Missiological Descriptions of Movements

The most common responses pertained to both biblical and missiological understandings of movements. These may seem like two different themes, but they were often tied together. Since missiology is inherently a biblical-theological "interdisciplinary discipline" (Priest, 2012), it was often not possible to discern between the two. For instance, one applicant wrote, "What are the Biblical foundations for a solid movements missiology?" Another answered, "I think a proper framing of movement methodology and its development from previously existing missiological ideas would be helpful - currently movements often come across as a new missiological fad...I think a more biblically and theologically sound explanation of movements would be helpful." Another example in this category succinctly explained, "It would be helpful for expat missionaries and national workers to understand the link between their daily efforts of making disciples and the movement of the Holy Spirit among the masses, both theologically and empirically." As some of the current literature on movements comes across to some as promotional in nature, this theme points to the felt need in the missions community for a more robust biblical and missiological description of contemporary discipleship movements or, at the least, for deeper descriptions of movements because such descriptions are not widely known or are not perceived to be deep enough.

2. Identifying Best Practices and Effective Movement Strategies

Another significant theme that emerged from the responses was more pragmatic. Respondents wanted to know the "How to…?" of movements. For example, what are the "activities in early stages of multiplication, especially in areas with small numbers of churches and local believers?" Another person remarked, "What are the practical how to's of starting from zero or near zero?" Yet another person wrote simply, "How to identify bottlenecks/obstacles." While many books have been written to propose a prescriptive side of movement missiology, there seems to be a need to further explain the strategic side of movements and possibly a need for evidence that these strategies work. Although only 9.5% suggested this, it points also to the fact that some believe that the best research should determine the best practices to emulate. One response clarifies the presupposition that the search for best practices and strategies is what may catalyze new movements: "Although movements vary from one context to another (structural variations), I suspect the existence of some universal driving forces on which we can build to make movements both sustainable and transferable."

Additionally, two people mentioned they would like to see more research on the phenomenon of movements starting movements, "How to go beyond sustaining movements to cascading movements?" And yet, sustainability was also a theme, "How to sustain rapid movement expansion after the point of movement maturity?" Related to this discussion, seven also mentioned issues related to the difficulty of catalyzing movements in the Global North. For example, "What role do CPM strategies have in re-evangelizing secular Europe? Despite some successes, why are CPMs slower in the West than anywhere else?" Three people also mentioned the urban aspects of movements, "How does this work out in mega multicultural cities and in the West?" This was echoed by another applicant, "Why aren't we seeing as much movement in Western contexts? Anyone seeing fruit using movement principles in diaspora?"

3. Identifying Issues of Ecclesiology – Practical, Theological, and Spiritual

The theological nature and practical form of churches in movements were also considered important, as 18 people suggested this theme. Several simply remarked that "ecclesiology" was an issue that needed more study. Others, however, were more detailed, "The effectiveness of discipleship and leadership structures within movements for yielding mature churches that remain faithful to historic Christian orthodoxy while innovating church forms and approaches to multiplying." A related issue involved the category "Theological and Spiritual Maturity/Health of Disciples and Churches" which 12 people mentioned as a concern. One mentioned, "Healthy church formation is the biggest question. How do we make sure that churches are healthy with strong local leadership?" Another said, "How much do people in generations 5 and above really understand who Jesus is? What does theology look like in further generations?"

Additionally, nine people suggested more research on the relationship between traditional, previously established churches (sometimes referred to as "legacy churches") and microchurches (house churches or small churches meeting in places other than official church buildings) in movements, "Does DMM (simple churches) undercut and diminish traditional church models? What is/should be the role of traditional churches in DMM?" Another echoed the comments of others in this category, "How will these movements connect with the wider, global body of Christ?" Taken together, these ecclesiological themes were one of the most significant in this data. This indicates the priority of healthy church formation that applicants placed in the overall mission discourse on movements.

4. Training Movement Catalysts and Practitioners

Eighteen people suggested research around the theme of training and maturing of movement catalysts, which seldomly (four times) included the most appropriate forms of advanced theological training. For example, "What makes coaching effective? What are the principles of decentralized leadership that allow movements to thrive?" Another said, "What kind of formal and informal training is needed for leadership of such movements?" Missionaries and expatriate movement practitioners were also a focus of training, as there were nine suggestions to research specific models and methods for training. One person asked, "How to help churches and Christian organizations transition from traditional mode of thinking and implementing to a mindset that accepts movements to Christ as its modus operandi?" This theme also included the role of expatriates and near-culture movement practitioners, "What is the role of foreign workers in movements?" In movements themselves, training is inherent in a community of practice with frequent periods of missiological reflection. This contrasts highly with a "university" model of education that has existed in the West. There is still much to be discovered in the area of training.

5. Highlighting Contextual, Sociological, and Holistic Features of Movements

Both contextual and sociological issues featured prominently in the research suggestions. One applicant wrote, "What can one learn from sociology to stimulate the growth of movements?" Another asked, "What barriers of spread are there, i.e., in a complex sociological world how does the gospel spread and what are social networks like in intertwined urban and virtual environments?" Related was the idea for more descriptive research of movements, "I would like to see more qualitative research done through which the voice of those within the movements can be heard." Many indicated that contextual issues needed more research, "What is the importance of retaining cultural identity for new believers," including "the role of socio-religious identity and what it means for movements?" Another wrote, "I would love to see more on how movements change and morph in different cultures and nations." Along these lines, another said, "Identifying differences and nuances between different ministry contexts and understanding the pre-existing conditions for movements." Nine people also inquired into how movements lead to the holistic transformation of society. Together, this theme reflects the incarnational interests in movements, including how and why movements contribute to the common good and human flourishing.

6. Documenting Movements with Respect to Verification, Metrics, and Administration

While the vast majority of themes suggested thus far were more qualitative in nature, quantitative issues also featured, although they too might not strictly focus on "numbers." Several people raised questions about the metrics and verification of movements. For example, "How are some of the claims of movements verified and reported?" Other responses asked simply, "What are the metrics for health?" or "What are the best evaluation methods?" Furthermore, six people wanted to know how outside finances are used in movements, including the negative effects of using resources not local to the movement itself. For example, one respondent asked, "Financial sustainability. How many CPMs are actually being sustained without outside dollars?" While less prominent than the previous themes, these administrative concerns also open up several directions for research.

Beyond the Emic/Etic Dichotomy: First- and Second-Order Research

As the previous section demonstrated, at least six gaps of information emerged from this inquiry into movements research. However, as already noted, these applicants to the Movements Research Symposium were mostly white males. In a postcolonial world, this is inadequate; more work needs to be done to integrate the voices of both women and nonwhite males. Be that as it may, it might be helpful to discuss how emic (insider) and etic (outsider) considerations impact the concept of research. How do local research initiatives relate to outside research agendas? This section will highlight the problematic etic/emic distinction and propose an improved framework.

Beyond the Binary Towards Integration

With roots in (missionary) linguistic theory in the mid-twentieth century, the emic/etic distinction sought to classify two distinct standpoints from which an observer could describe behavior: either from the inside or the outside. This pragmatic solution sought to systematize the study of language and avoid complicated philosophical discussions (Pike, 1954). Various disciplines in the social sciences and the study of religion later incorporated the emic/etic dichotomy. During this long process, however, debates raged between the emic/etic distinction regarding "whether or not or not religious 'insiders' have privileged access to and understanding of religious matters" (Mostowlansky & Rota, 2020, p. 9). One of the problems was the simplistic, binary nature of the distinction represented by the conflation of emic with "insider' and etic with "outsider." The insider/outsider distinction is better understood in terms of a continuum rather than a dualism, especially considering the presence of reciprocity and collaboration between the two. Mostowlansky and Rota (2020) further propose that the distinction between first- and second-order observers can disentangle these issues:

> First-order observers appreciate the world according to a specific perspective. However, they are not reflexively aware of the fact that their point of view is contextually situated. Religious insiders can be equated to first-order observers who relate to the world on the basis of their religious convictions – for instance, the way they conceive of God or the sacred. Second-order observers, on the other hand, examine how first-order observers observe; that is, they appreciate the perspectival character of first-order observations and explore how and

why first-order observers uphold a certain perspective. Academics can also be first-order observers, just as religious practitioners can reflexively assume the position of second-order observers. But emic and etic are not synonymous with first- and second-order observations. Rather, emic and etic analyses are both the product of second-order observers, although they imply different standpoints. (Mostowlansky & Rota, 2020, p. 10)

In other words, all participants and observers have a certain perspective that gives their knowledge both privileges and limitations. By way of analogy, we might consider a sports match. The players may have a certain perspective that can be classified as both emic and first-order. However, certain players may not be involved in every play and may be considered as etic and second-order observers simultaneously. The coach or analyst (or fan) also has a perspective that the players may not be able to grasp from their position alone. This is why successful players often watch (as an etic observer) a second-order "game tape" of their emic performances. Both the players and the coach/analyst can offer first- and second-order observations, as long as the perspectives of the player and coach/analyst are appreciated for their "positionality" (Rowe, 2014).

Concerning CPMs, we need to explicitly state that those with an "emic" perspective function not simply as "informants" but also as active movement participants whose perspectives are valued and respected. Local movement catalysts and the leadership teams formed among their disciples are all players learning the way God is at work in their movements by actively "playing" under his guidance, often with coaching from near culture mentors and/or Westerners from the sidelines. These are learning-by-doing communities, apprenticing successive generations of players with lessons learned on the ground. Because this training is more caught than taught, and only partially written down, it is much less recognizable to traditional academic research inquiries. Especially due to the relative novelty of some of the contemporary CPM and DMM phenomena, extant missiological literature lacks robust second-order research on these movements. As a result, seminaries and the academy often do not give movements serious consideration – to the detriment of both seminaries and movements. Yet in another sense, second-order research of the recent CPM and DMM phenomena can perhaps serve as an intermediary step toward local practitioners taking the lead in actively formulating their own research agendas. Anecdotally, I talked with one highly fruitful East African movement catalyst about research agendas within the postcolonial white/brown issue. I asked him what types of research projects he considered most helpful for movements. After thinking for some time, he replied, "Research is what you [white] guys are good at; we're [Africans] good at catalyzing movements." He appealed to more collaboration as the answer. In the end, the ideal may be for local people to initiate research and raise the questions most relevant to them. However, as this section has shown, research by second-order observers is not irrelevant to the discussion and may serve as a seedbed for future research.

A Biblical Example and Current Mission Applications of First- and Second-Order Observations

Tim Martin of the Motus Dei Network's facilitation team (personal interaction) has suggested that Acts 15 might also demonstrate the first- and second-order observers' construction of knowledge, specifically as it relates to missiological research. The novelty of Gentiles turning to Jesus caused the early church to ask new questions, perhaps similar to CPMs among the least-reached today. Paul and Barnabas reported a first-order perspective to the Jerusalem Council, but they were not emic participants in Gentile contexts. Peter and James also contributed a second-order perspective that first-order, emic Gentile Christ-followers have benefited from ever since! Research on CPMs may similarly reflect on the important integration of these perspectives. The six research gaps discussed in the previous section were admittedly dominated by second-order perspectives, but that does not render the themes irrelevant to first-order or emic concerns.

We can identify numerous emerging examples of research integration happening today. For example, the mission agency New Generations (newgenerations.org) is training first-order participants for qualitative assessments on their own movements (Brown, 2020). The Lausanne Movement (Lausanne.org) has been connecting and training non-Western researchers, with many of them examining movements through a second-order perspective (CMIW, 2018). AMRI, the Alliance of Mission Researchers and Institutions, aims to increase the capability of all parts of the Christian mission research community worldwide to participate in mission research, interdisciplinary scholarship, and publication, especially noting that capacity for mission research is not evenly distributed in the Global Church. And Focus on Fruit (focusonfruit.org) has facilitated a learning community of indigenous movement catalysts who have used both quantitative and qualitative research methods to discern fruitful practices within their own ministries that can be applied locally by other teams and by field practitioners in other contexts (Larsen, 2018). These are just a few examples of the integration between first- and second-order and emic/etic perspectives that show the body of Christ working together and collaborating in movements research (1 Cor. 12:25-26).

Underutilized Research Methods

Newer and underutilized research methods also show promise for this integration of first- and second-order research. For example, a "social network analysis" (SNA) of individuals, groups, churches, or networks within church planting movements could benefit the missiological discourse and add new insights to both the theology and praxis of mission. SNA is "a collection of theories and methods that assumes that the behavior of actors (whether individuals, groups, or organizations) is affected by (1) their ties to others and (2) the networks in which they are embedded" (Everton, 2018, p. 49). The common practice of "Fruit Charts" (a graphic illustration of which churches have successively planted other churches) in many movements create visual records of the growth of these networks that encourage both intuitive shepherding insights as well as analytic reflection on how and where movements spread (Larsen, 2020, Chapter 4). SNA is a field of study that has arisen in the intersection of social psychology, social anthropology, and graph theory in mathematics (Prell, 2012, pp. 19–58). SNA could therefore be used to investigate the role that real-world social networking plays in the spread of church planting movements. Especially since SNA defies the qualitative/quantitative research distinction, it shows promise as a way to graphically illustrate the specific shape of social networks where the transmission of faith is more likely to occur.

Another promising tool is "action research" in which movement "practitioner-researchers" seek solutions to problems faced in catalyzing movements. In so doing, the role of a movement catalyst or practitioner can be transformed from that of a "technician" to that of a "facilitator." In other words, starting a movement is not the implementation of a formula to fix a problem but involves bringing people together to address a challenge. This conceptual vision "advocates the use of contextually relevant procedures formulated by inquiring and resourceful practitioners" (Stringer, 2013, p. 3). Catalyzing movements is in itself a process of learning and research itself contributes to this learning. But more importantly, action research privileges the praxis of the *researched* over the theory of the *researcher* (Hutcherson & Melki, 2018, p. 234), thus prioritizing local research initiatives and properly setting expectations for second-order observers. Focus on Fruit, previously mentioned, begins their coaching of participants in movements using "Transformational Dialogue" that has this action research concept built into the process of catalyzing movements (Larsen, 2020, Chapter 1).

However, even considering these promising new approaches to research, further philosophical issues remain that are often not considered in missiological research; as a result, the quality of the research suffers.

Limitations of Qualitative Research in General

Young or inexperienced researchers (including missiologists with an axe to grind) often overstate the significance or conclusion of their study. Gary Thomas warns that the qualitative researcher should "not [be] out to prove something or to demonstrate that something is the case. Rather, you are looking to find the answer to a genuine question" (2017, p. 6). The evidence we find in qualitative research does not *solve* a case (we are not detectives), it merely *tells a story* as accurately as we can, admitting our bias. In this sense, social research provides "insights rather than generalisations... someone else will almost certainly find something very different from you, and this is to be expected" (2017, p. 140). In movements research, we need to be aware of the fallacy of objectivity. For qualitative research to be "valid," it need not be duplicated by another "objective" researcher. Combined with the idea of "positionality" previously discussed (i.e., first- and second-order observers), we can embrace subjectivity and not be ashamed or threatened by it (2017, p. 152). Learning what happens in and around movements may provide adequate data for decision-making in a local context but may or may not be a fruitful practice or best practice in another context.

Another common research fallacy to avoid is generalizing from insufficient evidence. For example, the idea of "theory" is used differently in research. By "theory," one might mean the term "Grand Theory" used mockingly by the sociologist C. Wright Mills to describe researchers who attempt to create universal explanations of the nature of man and society. Thomas notes that it is "a given that Grand Theory is not what is generally wanted in social research nowadays. You certainly will not be aiming to develop Grand Theory in your own research" (2017, p. 98). This needs constant evaluation in CPM research. Social science research offers many excellent theories, but in contrast to Grand Theories, they are called theories of the "middle-range" (Hedström & Udehn, 2009, p. 31) due to their limitations and contextual nature.

Avoiding Mistakes Associated with the Church Growth Movement

According to David Garrison, the concept of CPMs appears "to be a modification of Donald McGavran's landmark "People Movements" adapted to emphasize the distinctive of generating multiplying indigenous churches" (2011, p. 9). As a pioneer theorist for people movements, Donald McGavran asked in his book *Bridges of God* (1955), "How do *Peoples,* not just individuals, but clans, tribes, and castes, become Christian?" However, McGavran's original purpose of "church growth" within social networks led by unpaid leaders in house churches was later adapted for the quantitative goals of church enlargement for attractional and seeker-sensitive churches in the West. Lamenting this fact later in his life, McGavran preferred the term "church multiplication" over church growth (Fitts, 1993, p. 12).

While some are attempting to reconceive "church growth" for a new generation (Hunter III, 2009), the Church Growth Movement of the 1970s to 1990s was often described as technocratic and captive to a "fierce pragmatism" (Swartz, 2020, p. 108). McGavran actually began by only teaching non-American students because he was concerned that Westerners would individualize his theories and turn them into programs mistakenly claimed to be universally appropriate – it turns out he was correct. Further valid criticisms include appeals to religious consumerism and obsession with methods and formulas (Stetzer, 2006). Research on CPMs can avoid these tendencies by integrating non-Western postcolonial theological perspectives, more qualitative and contextually descriptive approaches to research, and avoiding the epistemological fallacies of positivism and naïve realism that were prevalent in earlier generations.

Summary

We long for the Global Church to one day share the Apostle Paul's "no place left" dilemma. Aided by awareness of current theories in research methodology, including an epistemological humility rooted in postcolonial sensitivities and collaboration, we have noted how different perspectives on research will shape research agendas and place values on different initiatives. Our research agendas should be built with a humble attitude about what we know, how we came to know it, and how our own perspectives enrich and limit our understanding. Different parts of the body of Christ may apply different methods and theoretical frameworks, but this article has argued for closer integration of this multi-faceted learning for the benefit of field ministries where God is allowing movements to grow. With that in mind, we noted six research gaps that can help improve the missiological discourse on church multiplication movements. These six gaps include:

1. Deepening Theological-Missiological Descriptions of Movements
2. Identifying Best Practices and Effective Movement Strategies
3. Clarifying Issues of Ecclesiology-Practical, Theological, and Spiritual
4. Training Movement Catalysts and Practitioners
5. Highlighting Contextual, Sociological, and Holistic Features of Movements
6. Documenting Movements with Respect to Verification, Metrics, and Administration

Research on CPMs needs to prioritize local initiatives, set realistic expectations for second-order observers and near-culture practitioners, and help missiologists see the value of phenomena that have been too easily dismissed as faddish. This research should therefore take a holistic view that integrates emic/etic and first- and second-order perspectives. We can and should find ways to be effective, empirical, educational, and edifying, all at the same time.

References

Bevans, S. B., Chai, T., Jennings, J. N., Jørgensen, K., & Werner, D. (Eds.). (2015). *Reflecting on and Equipping for Christian Mission* (Vol. 27). Regnum.

Brown, H. (2020). Celebrating 2 Years of Global Impact. *New Generations*. https://newgenerations.org/2020/07/celebrating-2-years-of-global-impact/

CMIW. (2018). *Research that Guides Kingdom Impact*. Community of Mission Information Workers. https://globalcmiw.org/node/64

Everton, S. F. (2018). *Networks and Religion: Ties that Bind, Loose, Build-up, and Tear Down*. Cambridge University Press.

Farah, W. (2020). Motus Dei: Disciple-Making Movements and the Mission of God. *Global Missiology*, *2*(17), 1–10.

Fitts, B. (1993). *Saturation Church Planting: Multiplying Congregations through House Churches*. Self-Published.

Garrison, D. (2004). *Church Planting Movements: How God Is Redeeming a Lost World*. WIGTake Resources.

Garrison, D. (2011). 10 Church Planting Movement FAQS. *Mission Frontiers*, *33*(2), 9–11.

Hedström, P., & Udehn, L. (2009). Analytical Sociology and the Theories of the Middle Range. In P. Bearman & P. Hedström (Eds.), *The Oxford Handbook of Analytical Sociology*. Oxford University Press.

Hunter III, G. G. (2009). *The Apostolic Congregation: Church Growth Reconceived for a New Generation*. Abingdon Press.

Hutcherson, C., & Melki, B. (2018). Action Research for Theological Impact: Reflections from an Arab Context. In P. Shaw & H. Dharamraj (Eds.), *Challenging Tradition: Innovation in Advanced Theological Education* (pp. 233–251). Langham.

Larsen, T. and A. B. of F. B. (2018). *Focus on Fruit!: Movement Case Studies and Fruitful Practices*. Self Published.

Larsen, T. and A. B. of F. B. (2020). *Core Skills of Movement Leaders: Repeating Patterns from Generation to Generation*. Self Published.

Long, J. (2020). 1% of the World: A Macroanalysis of 1,369 Movements to Christ. *Mission Frontiers, 42*(6), 37–42.

McGavran, D. (1955). *Bridges of God: A Study in the Strategy of Missions*. Wipf and Stock Publishers.

Mostowlansky, T., & Rota, A. (2020). Emic and Etic. In *The Cambridge Encyclopedia of Anthropology*. https://www.anthroencyclopedia.com/entry/emic-and-etic

Pachuau, L. (2018). *World Christianity: A Historical and Theological Introduction*. Abingdon Press.

Pike, K. L. (1954). *Language in Relation to a Unified Theory of the Structure of Human Behavior*. Summer Institute of Linguistics.

Prell, C. (2012). *Social Network Analysis: History, Theory and Methodology*. SAGE.

Priest, R. (2012). *What in the World Is Missiology!?* Missiology Matters. http://web.archive.org/web/20120427100553/http://www.missiology matters.com:80/2012/03/07/what-in-the-world-is-missiology/

Rowe, W. E. (2014). Positionality. In D. Coghlan & M. Brydon-Miller (Eds.), *The SAGE Encyclopedia of Action Research* (Vol. 1–2, pp. 627–628). SAGE.

Schreier, M. (2012). *Qualitative Content Analysis in Practice*. SAGE Publications.

Stetzer, E. (2006). The Evolution of Church Growth, Church Health, and the Missional Church: An Overview of the Church Growth Movement from, and Back to, Its Missional Roots. *Journal of the American Society for Church Growth, 17*(1), 87–112.

Stringer, E. T. (2013). *Action Research* (4th ed.). SAGE.

Swartz, D. R. (2020). *Facing West: American Evangelicals in an Age of World Christianity*. Oxford University Press.

Thomas, G. (2017). *How to Do Your Research Project: A Guide for for Students* (3rd ed.). SAGE Publications.

Wildemuth, B. M., & Zhang, Y. (2009). Qualitative Analysis of Content. In B. M. Wildemuth (Ed.), *Applications of Social Research Methods to Questions in Information and Library Science* (pp. 308–319). Libraries Unlimited.

About the Author

Dr. Warrick Farah serves with One Collective as a missiologist and theological educator in the Middle East. He is editor of the forthcoming William Carey Publishing text, *Motus Dei: The Movement of God and the Discipleship of Nations* (2021) as well as co-editor of *Margins of Islam: Ministry in Diverse Muslim Contexts* (2018). Warrick is the founder and a facilitator of the Motus Dei Network (https://motusdei.network) and is a researcher at the Oxford Centre for Mission Studies. Special thanks to the following people for their help with this article: DL, DC, SP, DO, AM, and JM.

GREAT COMMISSION
RESEARCH JOURNAL
2021, Vol. 13(2) 37-48

Sharing Jesus with Muslims: A Survey of Church Leaders in Africa

Akimana Canisius
Africa International University
Gordon Scott Bonham
One Challenge International

Abstract

A web survey of 34 pastors and other church leaders in 2020 who had met during graduate studies at Africa International University (AIU) was conducted to understand what is being done in Muslim evangelism in their home churches, primarily in East Africa. They generally characterized Muslims positively, as being made in the image of God, and as needing salvation through Jesus. They identified what they considered to be key differences between Muslims and Christians. Half of their churches made general evangelistic efforts, but most of these made no specific attempt to share the gospel with Muslims. Sharing the gospel with Muslims presents different challenges than sharing the gospel with people of other faiths. Their church members need a deeper understanding of the basic doctrines of the Trinity and salvation through Christ, along with training and tools on how to present the gospel to Muslims in a way they can hear, understand, and accept.

> *He said to them, "Go into all the world and preach the gospel to every creature."*
>
> *(Mark 16:15, NIV)*

The word of God - God the Father, God the Son, and God the Holy Spirit - makes it clear that Christians are called to share the gospel with everyone. The Bible says: "Therefore go and make disciples of all nations, baptizing them in the name of the Father and of the Son and the Holy Spirit, and teaching them to obey everything I have commanded you. And surely, I am with you always, to the very end of the age." (Matthew 28:19-20 NIV). Sometimes African Christians may forget that this mandate given to them applies to Muslims also. They claim, perhaps by ignorance, perhaps by experience, that Muslims are hard to preach to. Instead of going to them, Christians may complain about how Muslim hate Christians.

The gospel has been, and is being, preached to many people in Africa. Many disciples are made but few disciples are made among Muslims in East Africa. Why? This was the central question for a group of students from the Center for Islamic Studies at the Africa International University (AIU) who traveled from Nairobi, Kenya, to the Babati District, Manyara Region, Tanzania in the Spring of 2018. One of the authors (Akimana Canisius) was part of this student group and wrote to the other author (Gordon Bonham) soon afterward:

> *Muslims are very cooperative and love visitors. They welcome you to their houses, give you a seat, and listen to your message. It was amazing. Muslims are peaceful people and have a hunger for the gospel. In ten days, 30 Muslims gave their lives to Christ and others were calling us to stay another week. Only some challenges:*
>> *Churches there are very weak and have no program to reach Muslims. (We found Muslims 500 meters from the church, but never been visited by a single Christian.)*
>> *People speak only the Kiswahili language. No English there.*
>> *Pastors are not trained to win people, even non-Muslims.*
>> *People (Christians also) are very poor and non-educated.*

The lack of evangelism among Muslims may be due to the lack of training available to pastors and church members. "How, then, can they call on the one they have not believed in? And how can they believe in the one of whom they have not heard? And how can they hear without someone preaching to them?" (Romans 10:14 NIV).

Rev. Canisius decided to study the situation more deeply and to write his master's thesis on his findings (Canisius, 2020). Often using a translator, he conducted personal interviews with fifty leaders, ten from each of five Free Pentecostal Churches of Tanzania (FPCT) in Babati. After completing his thesis, he extended his research to other churches in East

Africa and across the world to have a clearer image of current practices concerning the evangelism of Muslims in African churches. Information from the pastors and other church leaders he knew during his studies at AIU, a melting-pot of students from more than thirty-four countries, could provide a broader image of what is being done in Muslim evangelism in their respective churches, most of which are in East Africa. Dr. Bonham had guided him on the interview design, sample procedure, and data analysis for his thesis. He suggested that using a web version of the original survey could be done even with the COVID-19 pandemic limiting interpersonal interviews. This paper presents findings from that web survey.

Methods

The web survey used Lime Survey software. Questions were in English, a language known to the 113 people invited to complete the survey. All except two of those invited to participate attended AIU. All were involved in ministry. Thirty-four of them (30%) responded to the survey between March 25 and April 10, 2020, with 28 providing useful information.

The home churches of 54% of the participants were in Kenya, 32% in other countries of East Africa (Burundi, Ethiopia, Rwanda, Tanzania, Uganda, and Zambia) and 14% in other countries (Canada, India, Ukraine, and the United States). Over half (57%) of their churches were in the major city of their country; 50% were pastors, 36% were other church leaders and members, and 14% had ministries not associated with a specific church (evangelist, missionary, or ministry coordinator). Most (79%) of the respondents were men, half (50%) were younger than 35 years of age, and 64% had been in their churches for more than ten years. Those from outside Africa were older and likely to be in ministries not associated with a specific church. Those with home churches in East Africa apart from Kenya tended to be from smaller places than those from Kenya or outside Africa and to have been in their home churches for longer periods.

Results

Attitudes toward Muslims

When asked what they thought about Muslims living in their communities, respondents gave answers that were classified into one or two of five underlying themes (Table 1).

Theme	Examples	Frequency
Muslims' need of salvation	"wrong faith" "how to reach them"	15
Positive characteristics	"good" "friendly" "strong beliefs"	12
Muslim's humanity	"image of God" "brothers and sisters"	9
Neutral characteristics	"size" "part of the community"	6
Negative characteristics	"enemies" "religious conflict"	4

Table 1: *Participants' Descriptions of Muslims*

The respondents were apparently thinking about Muslim's needs, characteristics, and humanity. None of them mentioned personal involvement with them nor the role of the Holy Spirit in engaging Muslims for Christ, indicating that Spirit-led interactions with Muslims were not salient in their thinking.

It appears that personal, regular interaction with Muslims influenced the participants' responses. Most of the respondents from villages and rural areas (80%) and small cities (57%) mentioned positive characteristics of Muslims, such as being friendly and good people who faithfully followed their religious beliefs, whereas only 19% of those whose churches are in the major city of the country did so. Conversely, those whose churches are in the major city are most likely (63%) to mention Muslims' need for salvation, compared to those from smaller cities (14%) and villages or rural areas (20%). Perhaps associated with personal relationships, women are more likely (67%) to mention positive characteristics of Muslims than men (27%). Most (59%) men mentioned Muslims' need for salvation in their responses, but none of the six women did. Half (50%) of the pastors and 16% of the non-pastoral church members said Muslims need salvation.

Respondents most often described the difference between Christians and Muslims in terms of their beliefs about the nature of God and Allah (14 respondents) and of Jesus and Mohamad (14 respondents). Often, these two went together. The good news about the Christian life and its benefits contrasted to the Muslim life (e.g., *true life and freedom, relationship with Jesus, assurance of eternal life*) was mentioned by nine respondents, frequently after they mentioned the nature of God or Jesus. Five respondents mentioned differences in beliefs without describing what the differences were. The remaining five respondents indicated that Muslims generally had a better lifestyle, better behavior, and a greater devotion to their religion than Christians.

Evangelism of Muslims

Evangelism Promoted by the Church. Although Christians may be trained in various forms of evangelism, what they practice may be quite different. Even if they are trained to share the gospel with Muslims, some may still simply reject the possibility that any Muslim would respond positively to the gospel.

This is in marked contrast to Jesus' attitude when he said that the harvest is plentiful, but the harvesters are few (Matt. 9:37). If Christians understand that Muslims do not know the gospel, it is their responsibility to explain it to them, to be a living witness of Jesus Christ and to fulfill the Great Commission.

Only five of the 34 respondents said their churches reach out specifically to the Muslim community: two through radio and TV broadcasts, two with specific ministries to Muslims, and one with specific training on Muslim evangelism. Four of these churches are the home churches of respondents under 35 and are in the major city of their country.

Ten respondents, however, were unaware of any effort in their church to share the gospel with Muslims. The remaining 19 respondents noted that their church encouraged interaction with Muslims through regular church activities which do not specifically target Muslims. These include door-to-door outreach, developing relationships with Muslims, praying and passing out tracts at events, and service ministries such as visiting patients in hospitals and aiding refugees.

Personal Evangelism. When asked about their personal involvement in Muslim evangelism, 12 respondents said they are personally involved in sharing Jesus with Muslims through a specific ministry or their work. At the other extreme, nine respondents said they are not involved in sharing the gospel. The remaining 12 indicated a desire to share the gospel with Muslims in the future and were more likely to share the gospel through personal relationships (7) than through specific program of evangelism (5). There was no clear relationship between the respondents' involvement in sharing Jesus with Muslims and whether their churches reached out to Muslims.

When asked how sharing Jesus with Muslims challenged them, respondents were challenged by Muslims' response to their evangelistic efforts and by finding an appropriate approach to the share the gospel with them. Some of the themes are found in Table 2.

Theme	Examples	Frequency
Doctrine and beliefs	"Which God is more powerful?" "They like disputes." "They don't accept Jesus as the Son of God."	7
Fear	"They run away." "Fear of their family if they convert" "Think Christians are their enemies"	5
Threats	"Killing and closing the church" "Taken to jail and court"	2
Knowledge	"Understand their worldview" "What I believe"	11
Strategy	"Only tell them about Jesus and wait for Jesus to show himself."	11

Table 2: *Challenges Faced when Sharing the Gospel with Muslims*

Hindrances to Muslim Evangelism. A question about what hinders a Muslim from following Jesus and a question about the factors that cause these hindrances identified both hindrances on the side of the Muslims and hindrances on the side of Christians. The primary hindrances for Muslims are the beliefs they have been taught from childhood, mentioned 11 times. Six respondents mentioned the importance of family relationships and that following Jesus would hurt the relationships. Six also mentioned the very real danger of persecution by the community or the state that could lead to imprisonment and death. Other hindrances mentioned include Muslim pride and a lack of knowledge about Christianity. Specific Christian theology that is contrary to Muslim beliefs was mentioned by 10 respondents, primarily the theology of the Trinity that identifies Jesus as part of the Godhead, and the doctrine of salvation through Jesus alone. The resurrection, the authority of the Bible, and its truthfulness were also among the theological hindrances.

Respondents also mentioned hindrances and limitations that Christians face when sharing their faith with Muslims, including their limited knowledge about the gospel, about Islam, and about how to share the gospel with a Muslim. Mentioned less frequently, but still, a major hindrance was the lifestyle practices of Christians—the divisions among them, the incongruence between their words and behavior, their denigration of Muslim culture, and Christians' lack of love. Three respondents mentioned the need to let the Holy Spirit work in Muslim hearts and focus on prayer rather than on strategies to bridge the vast differences between the two faiths. Other hindrances include Christians fearing Muslims, lack of follow-up if a Muslim shows interest and starts following Jesus, and Christianity being so strongly identified as a foreign (Western) religion.

All six of the female respondents indicated hindrances on the part of Muslims, with four of them saying it was their beliefs; none suggested persecution as a hindrance. Only two females (33%) suggested Christian knowledge and lack of seeking the Spirit's involvement as hindrances. More than half of male respondents (59%) indicated hindrances on the part of Muslims and many of them noted the persecution that a Muslim who indicated an interest in Jesus would face. Unlike females, most (86%) of the males also indicated hindrances associated with Christians' lack of theological knowledge, particularly about the Trinity.

Means Used to Evangelize Muslims. Most of the respondents (28) had experience sharing Jesus or talking about the gospel with Muslims. Participants were asked to identify the tools they used when evangelizing Muslims. The Bible was used by 21 of them, with 9 using it as their only tool and 12 used the Bible along with other material (e.g., tracts, pamphlets, materials about their church, and the Qur'an). A few used other methods that included sports, prayer during hospital visitations, drama, and singing.

Another question asked about the ways that the participants prepared for sharing the gospel with Muslims. The responses included preparing material to distribute and preparing oneself through prayer, Bible reading, fasting, discussing issues with others, and reading material used by Muslims. In general, those who listed more tools also listed more ways of preparing for the sharing the gospel.

Responsibilities of Churches

Participants were asked what they believed that their churches should do to evangelize Muslims. The answers respondents gave to this question clustered into four goals, from motivation to action. Respondents often included multiple ideas in their responses. The main themes are presented in Table 3.

Goal	Theme	Examples	Frequency
Motivation	Inspiration	"Awareness and mobilization of Muslim evangelism" "Reach out to Muslims; they are our brothers."	3
	Relationships	"Invite them to a private place." "Practice unconditional love to them."	9
Learning	Studying	"Understanding the Trinity very well" "in-depth study of the Bible"	8
	Training	"Equip and teach church more on Muslim evangelism." "How to handle a Muslim mind conditioned since childhood"	13
Planning		"Prepare well." "Decide to visit them."	6
Action	Prayer	"Invest more in praying."	5
	Support	"Support human needs." "Schools to attract students"	3

Table 3: *Challenges Faced when Sharing the Gospel with Muslims*

The characteristics of the respondents were not related to whether they thought their church needed to inspire members to share the gospel.

Those from Kenya and outside Africa reported less need for studying and training than those from other East Africa countries (89% vs. 36%), and pastors were more likely than church members to think the church needed to teach and train members for sharing the gospel (79% vs. 30%). Men were the only ones to mention planning, and those whose home church is in the major city of the country mentioned planning much more frequently than those from smaller places (31% vs 6%).

Costs Associated with Muslim Evangelism

Because there can be negative consequences associated with sharing the gospel with Muslims, the survey ended with a question about the cost of sharing the gospel with Muslims. The respondents recorded costs that we classified into two categories: Preparation Costs, which occur before one shares the gospel with Muslims, and Resulting Costs, which occur after.

The most frequently reported Preparation Cost was Time, identified by ten respondents - the time it took to prepare, to make contacts, and develop relationships that would be necessary to share the gospel. The financial cost of training for Muslim evangelism and the financial cost due to time taken away from salaried work or to pay for transportation were identified by six respondents. Mentioned by a few where the social costs of having their purposes misunderstood, having to assume responsibility for sharing, and having to demonstrate their good intentions by good deeds, such as visiting people in the hospital or meeting physical needs.

The most frequently mentioned Resulting Cost was death, either for the Christian for having tried to proselytize Muslims or for the Muslim if the Muslim accepted the gospel. Sharing the gospel might also cost time and money for following up with an open person, perhaps even including the responsibility to house him or her if the Muslim community rejects the convert. The psychological costs of suffering and discouragement due to being insulted or rejected in their efforts to share the gospel were also mentioned, especially in light of the biblical responsibility to endure. One participant also mentioned that a Christian may risk rejection from other Christians who do not support his or her efforts to reach Muslims.

Discussion

Muslims need salvation. Created in God's image, they need to know God to experience true and everlasting life. If African churches are not ready to reach out to Muslims in the 21st century, how can we fulfill the Great Commission in our lifetime? As it is written, "How beautiful are the feet of those who bring good news" (Romans 10:15, NIV). But how can they bring the good news if they are not sent out and prepared to bring it in a way that Muslims can hear, understand, and accept? Evangelizing Muslims should be viewed as sharing the good news of Christ to the lost rather than an attempt to present a better or alternative religion. The gospel "is the power of God for salvation of everyone who believes" (Romans 1:16, NIV).

The responses of the 34 Africans surveyed were characterized by common themes about sharing the gospel with Muslims, even though they reflected experiences in many countries, in different sized communities with various denominational affiliations, and of people with differing church responsibilities. They generally identified Muslims as having positive human characteristics, made in the image of God, and needing salvation through Jesus. Only four mentioned negative characteristics of Muslims, so prejudice or fear does not seem to be a major barrier. Most said their churches had general evangelistic efforts but made few attempts to share the gospel specifically with Muslims. They could generally identify key differences between Muslims and Christians in beliefs about the nature of God, Allah, Jesus, and Muhammad.

These church leaders identified challenges and hindrances in sharing the gospel, some coming from the Muslims' background and community and others due to basic Christian doctrines such as the Trinity and salvation through Christ alone. Church members' understanding of these doctrines and how to present them were hindrances, often not helped by the behavior and divisions among Christians. The Bible was the primary tool used in sharing the gospel, although there was little or no recognition that Muslims may not view the Bible as being relevant. Some used tracts or pamphlets that might help Muslims better hear the gospel message.

Churches need to motivate and train their members to share the gospel with Muslims, plan Muslim evangelism, and then take concrete steps to carry out the plans. Christians should conduct themselves in a manner worthy of the gospel of Christ so that the non-believers will be drawn to Christ by the testimony of their changed lives.

Different churches may need to begin or focus on different steps in this progression. An earlier survey of ten leaders in five different churches in a specific urban area in Africa showed that each church was in a different place (Canisius and Bonham, 2020). Most of the leaders at two of the churches felt that training and planning were needed. Those at another church mainly said they needed to pray. One of the churches had tried Muslim evangelism unsuccessfully and blamed Muslims rather than their lack of training or preparation. The importance of pastoral leadership was mentioned by a few of the leaders who felt that the senior pastor was hindering members from sharing the gospel with Muslims. In the present study, one-third of the respondents indicated the need to motivate church members to interact with Muslims and develop relationships, and half indicated the need for church members to learn more about the gospel message and how to share it.

The results from of this present study speak loudly and reinforce the findings from previous research. Church leaders believe that Muslims need salvation. All Kenyan pastors in charge of local churches in this study clearly responded that Muslims need salvation, as did all the evangelists, missionaries, and area coordinators. In contrast, church members and those from smaller communities emphasized favorable aspects of the Muslims they knew rather than their need for salvation. This means that the church leaders know that they need to share the gospel with Muslims, but this may not be the priority of the typical church member.

The two studies have found that many African churches do not make Muslim evangelism a priority. This matters a lot for the evangelical church in East Africa, a region where so many Muslims are found, and in the world globally. None of the leaders in these two studies indicated that their churches were trained in Muslim evangelism. Many of these churches do general evangelism through social services, open worship services, and door-to-door visitation, but not with a focus on Muslims. This is a major drawback. Some churches and church members may not interact with Muslims at all. Church members need both motivation and training in Muslim evangelism, beginning with the leaders of these churches.

This current research used an online tool that did not allow direct interaction with the respondents but did permit a greater geographical representation than the earlier study, which was based on direct contact between the researcher and the interviewees. In the earlier research, Canisius was able to record information beyond that evoked by his initial interview questions. He was able to communicate with respondents face-to-face, probing their fears and doubts with clarifying questions and interpreting the expressions on their faces. However, both types of research show that many congregants are not aware of how to share the gospel with Muslims. They also show that different churches in different locations may need evangelism training with slightly different emphases based on the local Muslim environment and the local church's missional view.

We recommend additional research on how African churches train, or need to train, members to reach out to Muslims. This should take place in individual churches to best fit the need of the specific context. Such research also needs to be done in other countries and cultures, with churches of different denominations and different sizes to better understand the preparedness of churches in reaching out to Muslims with the gospel. This would enable training to be contextualized to each location. Yet, churches cannot wait for more extensive research. Denominational and network leaders should look at their own churches and introduce training programs to teach church members how to evangelize Muslims. Church leaders must also remind their congregations of the need to interact with Muslims, develop relationships that will allow them to share the gospel, and be trained in ways that have proven to be effective.

The commitment of local churches around the globe, and of Christian organizations, to Muslim evangelism must become more visible than in the past. Our main purpose as Christians is to glorify God by fulfilling His mandate to reach out to unreached people, including Muslims. The church exists because God exists. An inactive state is not appropriate for a born-again Christian.

References

Canisius, A. (2020). Factors affecting Muslim evangelism: A study of Free Pentecostal Church of Babati Council Town, Tanzania. *World Journal of Research and Review, 11*(4), 52-57.

Canisius, A. and Bonham, G. (2020). *Church factors affecting Muslim evangelism.* Bonham Research.

Christy, M. W. (2009*). The role of the Holy Spirit in Missions from a biblical perspective.* Southwestern Baptist Theological Seminary.

Leafe, S. K. (2017). *A practical approach to evangelizing Muslims.* Scriptel.org

About the Authors

Rev. Akimana Canisius earned his master's in Missions Studies-Islamic Emphasis from Africa International University, Nairobi, Kenya. He is married and involved in research.

Dr. Gordon Scott Bonham earned his doctoral degree in sociology from the University of Michigan, USA. He is a research associate with One Challenge International.

GREAT COMMISSION
RESEARCH JOURNAL
2021, Vol. 13(2) 49-70

Innovativeness and Church Commitment: What Innovations Were Most Important During the Pandemic?

Anna Covarrubias, David R. Dunaetz
and Wendi Dykes McGehee
Azusa Pacific University

Abstract

The COVID-19 pandemic created an unprecedented need for innovations in churches around the world. Organizational innovativeness, a precursor of successful innovations in organizational contexts, is rarely studied in churches. This study of American church attenders (N = 244) found that perceived innovativeness of churches (conceived of as the elements of a church's culture which promote innovation, specifically, creativity, organizational openness, future orientation, risk-taking, and proactiveness) was a very strong predictor of church commitment (conceived of as intentions to stay in the church, r = .60, p < .001). Of the moderators examined in this study (membership tenure, age of participant, church size, and gender), only gender moderated this relationship; the relationship between perceived innovativeness and church commitment was stronger for females than for males. This suggests that innovations that facilitated relationship development and relationship maintenance had the greatest impact on church commitment during the pandemic.

Gordon Penfold, Guest Editor

Beginning in March 2020, a combination of general fear and government regulations forced churches in the United States and throughout the world to halt face-to-face meetings, whether for worship, teaching, evangelism, service, or fellowship. Such a disruption in church programs was unprecedented in recent memory and created a more urgent need for ministry innovation than these churches had ever previously experienced. Although the aftermath of the pandemic is not yet fully understood, some churches will likely withstand the pandemic more successfully than others (Rainer, 2020; Whitesel, 2020). Changes made within a church during the pandemic (via innovations such as moving small groups and youth ministries online) will likely be a major factor contributing to the long-term outcomes that the church will experience.

An important outcome of the pandemic that concerns virtually all churches is whether members will continue to be committed to their pre-pandemic church, will they leave the church to start attending elsewhere, or will they not return to church at all? This study explores whether perceived church innovativeness (the elements of organizational culture that promote innovations in a church; Ruvio et al., 2014) is related to commitment to one's church during the pandemic. Given that church members are often reputed for being resistant to change (Barna, 1993; Neighbour, 1973; Penfold & Taylor, 2020), it is possible that innovativeness is viewed negatively by church members and decreases their commitment to the church as they see the old and familiar threatened by the new and unfamiliar. Yet it is also quite possible that innovativeness has a positive effect on church members, increasing their commitment to the church as they see the church respond creatively and effectively to the challenges faced during the pandemic.

Organizational Innovativeness in Churches

Organizational Innovativeness is an important concept actively studied in organizational psychology, management, and business, but is rarely studied in churches. The term *innovation* is derived from the Latin word *novus* "new." In organizational contexts, it can be defined as a new and beneficial process, idea, or product within a group, organization, or wider society (Choi & Choi, 2014; Powell & Pepper, 2018; Ruvio et al., 2014). From a theological point of view, innovations initiated by both God and humans are important. For example, for humans, innovation is an important aspect of worship (Psalm 96:1). Moreover, it is fundamental to Christ's redemptive work; when individuals place their faith in Christ, through God's work of regeneration, a new creation emerges and all is made new (2 Cor. 5:17), as will occur also with all of creation at Christ's return (Rev. 21:5).

Innovativeness, an aspect of an organization's culture, supports innovative processes over time and can be described as the willingness, capacity, and openness to innovate (Hult et al., 2004; Hurley et al., 2005; Powell & Pepper, 2018; Ruvio et al., 2014). Innovativeness can be seen in the thinking of the apostle Paul when he speaks of a "great door for effective work" being opened (I Corinthians 16:9, NIV) and "an open door for our message" (Colossians 4:3, NIV). These passages reflect the heart of a God (as well as the *Missio Dei*) who desires the effects of the gospel to progress, expand, and grow.

Organizational Innovativeness has sometimes been viewed as the number of innovations an organization produces (Garcia & Calantone, 2002; Salavou, 2004; Wang & Ahmed, 2004). Others consider innovativeness to be an aspect of organizational culture reflecting a climate within an organization that is open, willing, and supportive of the continuous generation of ideas, products, or change (Hult et al., 2004; Hurley et al., 2005; Salavou, 2004; Wang & Ahmed, 2004). Simply recognizing the need for innovation and integrating this need into the culture is likely to contribute to innovation (Van de Ven, 1986). In effect, an innovation is the product or idea that is generated while innovativeness is the culture that supports innovation and innovators.

Ruvio and colleagues (2014) have developed a five-dimensional model of organizational innovativeness. Rather than assuming that the number of innovations produced by an organization represents their innovativeness, this model describes five aspects of culture that characterize innovativeness: creativity, organizational openness, future orientation, risk-taking, and proactiveness.

Creativity

Woodman, Sawyer, and Griffin (1993) describe the end product of organizational-level and group-level creativity as "the creation of a valuable, useful new product, service, idea, procedure or process by individuals working together in a complex social system" (p. 293). While group creativity is not simply the sum of the individual group members' creativity, group composition, characteristics, and process factors contribute to group creativity (Woodman, Sawyer, & Griffin, 1993). Antecedents to group creativity include leadership, cohesiveness, group composition, and group structure (King & Anderson, 1990). Research around these factors suggests that creative outcomes are more frequently generated when the leadership is collaborative and democratic (in contrast to autocratic), the structure is less formal and mechanistic, and group members are characterized by cognitive and functional diversity (Woodman, Sawyer, & Griffin, 1993). Similarly, creativity at the individual level (a necessary part of organizational creativity) depends on group and organizational culture which is influenced by how the social, contextual, and environmental characteristics of the group and organization interact with one another.

A potential hindrance to group creativity is groupthink (Janis, 1982). Groupthink characterizes decision-making when consensus and harmony are top priorities. With these priorities, group members discourage external influences and critical thought to enter the discussion, thus reducing the potential for creativity (Janis, 1982).

The concept of creativity is a central theme of the early chapters of Genesis describing the creation of the world. From there, this Creator of the world is revealed to be the God whom his people are to love and serve. Yet the creativity of God is not limited to the world as we now know it; it also characterizes his actions at the consummation of time, "For behold, I create new heavens and a new earth" (Is. 65:17, NASB).

Organizational Openness

Organizational openness is an aspect of organizational culture characterized by flexibility and adaptability in response to new ideas and changes (Ruvio et al, 2014; Hurlet et al., 2005). Flexibility and adaptability are most likely to occur when the need for new ideas and actions is recognized (Van de Ven, 1986). Organizational openness to a specific change consists of two parts (1) the willingness of the organization to support the new idea or change and (2) positive feelings of the employees concerning the potential consequences of the innovation (Wanberg & Banas, 2000).

Although openness to false teaching and doctrine is strongly discouraged in the Bible (e.g., Gal. 1:6-9), openness to Spirit-led ecclesial changes characterizes much of the New Testament (e.g., the Jerusalem Council in Acts 15 and Paul's exhortations in his epistles). This need for openness to change continues today; Powell and colleagues (2012) found that the perception of a church's openness to innovation attracts newcomers and promotes the growth of the church.

Future Orientation

Rather than relying on past experiences to predict future success, a future orientation looks toward possibilities and envisions what may lie ahead (Ford, 2002). Vision casting, goal setting, and the creation of a culture that focuses on the future are precursors of innovation because they encourage creativity and outside-the-box thinking (Ford, 2002; Gavetti & Levinthal, 2000). An organizational culture characterized by a future orientation paves the way for radical innovation (as opposed to incremental innovation) because vision casting and goal setting encourage people to think of the broadest range of possibilities rather than the gradual improvement of existing products, processes, and services (Christensen, 2013).

A biblical example of goal setting requiring outside-the-box thinking can be found in Mark 2:1-12 where a group of men brought their paralyzed friend to be healed by Jesus. After realizing that access to Jesus was not feasible because of a large crowd, they dug a hole in the roof of the building and lowered their friend to Jesus. Jesus, being impressed by their faith as expressed in their determination to reach their goal through an innovative technique, healed the man both physically and spiritually.

Risk-Taking

A culture of risk-taking is an important aspect of innovative organizations (Ruvio et al, 2014). Risk-taking can be defined as the degree to which organizations are willing to make commitments with unsure outcomes in attempting to realize their goals and vision (Caruana et al., 2002; Lumpkin & Dess, 1996; Miller & Friesen, 1978). Genuine risk includes the threat of a poor outcome (March & Shapira, 1987), a threat that is unacceptable in many organizations and thus hinders innovation. Risk-taking organizations give permission to fail and encourage experimentation in order to promote creativity and innovation (Dykes, 2018; Kelley & Kelley, 2013).

The woman who anointed Jesus' feet with perfume at Simon's house serves as a biblical example of risk-taking (Matt. 26: 6-13). This act could have resulted in her ostracism from the community. She was criticized by the disciples for her actions, yet Jesus viewed it as a beautiful sacrifice and predicted that her story would be told throughout the course of time.

Proactiveness

The attempt to lead rather than follow competitors (Miller & Friesen, 1983) is a mindset that helps to frame the definition of proactiveness. Proactive behavior involves taking the initiative to act, along with experimenting with ideas and anticipating and acting upon future possibilities (Dess et al., 1997; Rauch et al., 2009). This idea of initiative, a tangible action element, is central to the development of innovative behavior within the organization (Dess et al., 1997) and requires leaders to motivate individuals in their span of care toward implementation (Caruana et al, 2002). Proactiveness is a major biblical theme. For example, in the book of Proverbs, the ant illustrates the importance of proactiveness as it stores food in summer in preparation for the winter (Prov. 6:6-11). Similarly, in the New Testament, Paul calls for proactive behavior by exhorting Christians to "put on the full armor of God" in preparation for standing firmly during their struggles against spiritual forces of evil (Eph. 6:10-18, NIV).

Church Commitment

The disruptions caused by the pandemic have caused many church leaders to wonder if their church would come out of the pandemic weakened and diminished once the restrictions are fully removed. It is quite likely that some, if not most churches, will find that some attenders will no longer be participating in church life as they did pre-pandemic, either because they will have lost the habit of going to church or because they will have chosen to start attending other churches. Such changes are a reflection of a person's *church commitment*, "a Christian's sense of attachment and loyalty to the church that he or she attends most frequently" (Dunaetz, Cullum, and Barron, 2018, p. 126).

Church commitment is important from both a practical and a theological point of view. On a practical (or administrative) level, low church commitment can lead to a person leaving a church which may hurt a church financially and weaken the church's ministries in which the person participated. Theologically and from a spiritual point of view, church commitment is also important. Commitment to the Lord is a central biblical value (Deut. 6:5; Matt 22:37). Such a commitment should be very high, greater than one's commitment to one's family (Luke 14:26-27), a commitment held steadfastly and unwaveringly (Luke 9:62). As the church is the body of Christ (Rom. 12:5; I Cor. 3:17), commitment to Christ can be manifested in a commitment to his church. Church commitment can even be considered a visible (but imperfect) proxy for commitment to, and faith in, Christ (James 2:14-26).

In organizational psychology, the commitment an employee has to an organization is known as *organizational commitment* (Allen & Meyer, 1990; Cohen, 2013; Meyer & Allen, 1991) which can be defined as "an employee's sense of attachment and loyalty to the work organization with which the employee is associated" (Cohen, 2013, p. 526). This is conceptually similar to church commitment and variations of organizational commitment scales have been adapted to measure church commitment (Dunaetz & Bocock, 2020; Dunaetz, Cullum, et al., 2018; Dunaetz et al., 2021). Organizational commitment is important because its consequences include a greater willingness to invest oneself into one's work, higher quality work, greater satisfaction with one's work, and lower turnover and absenteeism (Cohen, 2013). In churches, greater church commitment predicts greater ministry involvement of lay people (Dunaetz & Bocock, 2020).

The antecedents of organizational commitment include shared values with leaders, satisfaction with one's responsibilities, and a desire to maintain relationships with one's coworkers (Cohen, 2013). Among church attenders, tenure (how long a person has attended a church), pastoral humility (vs. pastoral narcissism), and church size (commitment is higher in smaller churches than larger churches) are, at least sometimes, all predictors of church commitment (Dunaetz, Cullum, & Barron, 2018). Similarly, the degree to which a person shares values with the church predicts church commitment, at least in smaller churches, but to a lesser degree in larger churches (Dunaetz et al., 2021).

This study will examine if, and to what degree, church innovativeness predicts church commitment.

Hypotheses

Organizational innovativeness in churches may be viewed negatively because of church members' resistance to change. If this is the case, organizational innovativeness will likely predict lower church commitment. Yet organizational innovativeness may be viewed positively because of the greater responsiveness it permits to church members' needs in new contexts. In this case, organizational innovativeness will predict an increase in church commitment. This study will test which of these two attitudes towards innovation has dominated during the COVID-19 pandemic. Thus, the first hypothesis is:

H₁: Organizational innovativeness in churches will be correlated to church commitment.

If this exploratory hypothesis is supported, we will be able to determine if church innovativeness has a positive or negative effect on members' commitment to the church.

If church innovativeness impacts church members' commitment to the church, we would also like to know under what conditions this is most likely to be true. Is it more true in small churches than large churches? Is it more true for men than for women? Is there a difference between older church members and younger church members? This study examines whether certain conditions impact the relationship between innovativeness and church commitment. Specifically, we examine the impact of the size of the church, the age of the person providing information about his or her church, how long the person has been attending the church (tenure), and the person's sex. The second hypothesis is thus:

H_2: The relationship between organizational innovativeness and church commitment will be moderated by church size, participant's age, participant's tenure, and/or participant's sex.

If this hypothesis is supported, it may provide insight into what types of innovation have been most important during the pandemic. It may also provide clues to the nature of effective ministry in a post-pandemic world.

Method

In order to test these two hypotheses, an electronic survey was used to collect data during the pandemic from adults who attended evangelical or other protestant churches.

Participants

Invitations were sent out to members of the first two authors' social networks through social media, email, and texting. Participants were required to be 18 years or older and attend an evangelical or other protestant church. In order to detect correlations of at least $r = .15$ with a statistical power of 80%, the target sample size was 347 participants. However, only 258 participants were able to be recruited. Of these 258 participants, 244 provided usable data; there were 14 participants whose data showed little or no variation in responses indicating that they did not read and respond to the items thoughtfully.

Measures

After providing their informed consent to participate in the study, participants received a series of items that measured the variables required to test the hypotheses and demographic information.

Church Innovativeness. Based on Ruvio et al.'s (2014) 21-item organizational innovativeness scale, 9 items were chosen which were especially appropriate for churches. These 9 items were modified slightly for church contexts to create the Church Innovativeness Scale (Appendix A). Participants indicated their agreement to each of the items on a 5-point Likert scale ranging from 1 = Strongly Disagree to 5 = Strongly Agree. Sample items include "My church is open and responsive to change" and "The leaders are always seeking new opportunities for the church." Cronbach's (1951) coefficient of reliability for this measure was excellent, $α = .91$.

Church Commitment. Although a participant's church commitment, like organizational commitment, can be measured as a multidimensional construct (Dunaetz, Cullum, et al., 2018; Meyer & Allen,

1991), for this study, church commitment was conceptualized as a unidimensional construct focusing on the person's desire to stay or leave the church based on how well the church corresponds to the person's needs and expectations. Based on Bothma and Roodt's (2013) Turnover Intention Scale (TIS-6), items were modified to describe intentions to stay at one's church (Appendix B). Participants indicated their agreement to the six items on a 5-point Likert scale ranging from 1 = Strongly Disagree to 5 = Strongly Agree. Sample items include "I often look forward to going to church" and "I often think about finding another church that will better suit my needs" (reverse scored). Cronbach's (1951) coefficient of reliability for this measure was excellent, $\alpha = .89$.

Tenure. The time that a person had been attending his or her church (tenure) was measured with a single question, "How long (in years) have you attended your current church? Enter 0 if you've attended for less than 6 months." The average tenure of participants was 8.85 years.

Age. The age of participants was measured using a single item asking their age. The average age of participants was 39.40 years.

Gender. Participants indicated their gender with a single item asking their gender. The majority of participants (66.5%) were female.

Church Size. Participants were asked to indicate how many people attend their church each week and were given a list of 8 choices ranging from "Less than 20" to "More than 2000". The median church size was "201-500".

Race/Ethnicity. Participants were asked to indicate their race or ethnicity if they so desired. Reflecting the Southern California location of the authors, 48.8% of participants identified as White/Caucasian, 35.3% as Latino, 5.1% as Black/African American, and 3.9% as Asian.

Results

Descriptive Statistics

The mean, standard deviation, and range of scores for the variables measured in this study are presented in Table 1. Church innovativeness and church commitment were calculated for each individual by averaging the scores of the items used to measure these constructs (after appropriately unreversing the reverse-scored items; Appendices A and B) so that higher scores indicated higher church innovativeness and greater church commitment. This resulted in scores that could, and indeed did, range from 1.00 to 5.00 with 3.00 as the neutral point. In general, participants saw both their churches' innovativeness ($M = 3.51$) and their commitment to their church ($M = 3.70$) as above the neutral point.

Measures	*M*	*SD*	Range
Church Innovativeness	3.51	0.88	1.00 – 5.00
Church Commitment	3.70	0.93	1.00 – 5.00
Tenure	8.85	8.84	0 - 45
Church Size	4.93	2.29	1 - 8
Age	39.40	12.16	18 - 79

Note: N = 244.

Table 1. *Descriptive Statistics*

The table of correlations of the main variables in the study is presented in Table 2. Note that neither church innovativeness nor church commitment were significantly related to the demographics of the participants (tenure, age, gender); perceived church innovativeness and church commitment did not vary between old and young, new members and old-timers, or between men and women. However, they did vary with church size. Larger churches were seen to be more innovative than smaller churches. Moreover, church commitment was higher in large churches rather than in small churches during the pandemic; this is in contrast to a lower level of commitment sometimes seen in larger churches relative to smaller churches (Dunaetz, Cullum, et al., 2018; von der Ruhr & Daniels, 2012).

	1	2	3	4	5	6
1. Church Innovativeness	--					
2. Church Commitment	.597***	--				
3. Tenure (years)	-.124	-.065	--			
4. Church Size	.134*	.166**	.034	--		
5. Age	.002	-.008	.271***	-.066	--	
6. Gender	.042	-.039	.006	-.126	.049	--

Note: $*p < .05, **p < .01, *** p < .001$, two-tailed. *N* = 244.
For gender, 1 = male, 2 = female

Table 2. *Correlations of Main Variables*

Hypothesis Testing

The first hypothesis in this study predicted that church innovativeness would predict church commitment, although the direction of this relationship was not known. This hypothesis was supported, $r(242) = .60$, $p < .001$, two-tailed. Specifically, greater perceived church innovativeness strongly predicted greater church commitment. During the pandemic, innovativeness was viewed very positively; church member's resistance to change does not appear to have affected their church commitment during this period where the felt need for innovation was high.

The second hypothesis predicted that the relationship between church innovativeness and church commitment would be moderated by the demographic characteristics of the participants or their churches. This hypothesis was not supported for participants' tenure, age, or church size. There was no significant difference in this relationship for people of different ages, for people who had attended their church for different periods of time, or for different sized churches; in all these comparisons, the strength of the relationship between church innovativeness and church commitment did not significantly vary ($ps > .05$).

However, there was a significant difference in the relationship between church innovativeness and church commitment when comparing men to women. Gender was a significant moderator of this relationship, $B = .25$, $SE = .12$, $t = 2.11$, $p = .036$ (Figure 1). The relationship between innovativeness and church commitment was stronger in women than in men. In churches with high innovativeness, church commitment is high, and women's church commitment is somewhat higher than men's church commitment. However, in churches with low innovativeness, church commitment is low and women's church commitment is much lower than men's church commitment.

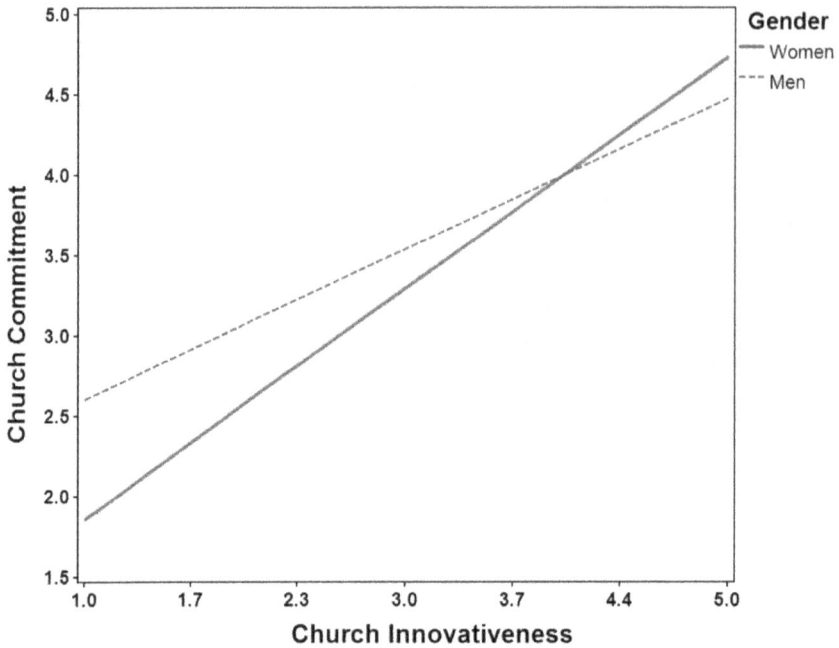

Figure 1. *Moderation of the Relationship Between Church Innovativeness and Church Commitment by Gender.*
The relationship between church innovativeness and church commitment is significantly stronger in women (solid line) than in men (dotted line) because the line for women has a steeper slope. The difference between men's and women's church commitment is especially noticeable in churches with low innovativeness. Women's church commitment is much lower than men's church commitment in churches that are low in innovativeness.

Discussion

This study explored whether church innovativeness, defined as the elements of a church's culture that promote innovation (specifically, creativity, organizational openness, future orientation, risk-taking, and proactiveness), was related to church commitment during the COVID-19 pandemic. A very strong positive correlation was found between church innovativeness and church commitment; the more people perceived their church to be innovative, the stronger their commitment was to stay in the church.

This study also examined possible factors (moderators) that would change this relationship. The strength of this relationship did not significantly change with church size, participant age, or participant tenure in the church. It was constant across all these variables. However, it was much stronger for women than for men, suggesting that innovations that responded to women's priorities (relative to men's priorities) were especially influential during the pandemic.

The Importance of Innovativeness

This study provides evidence that innovativeness was very important in keeping people committed to the church during the pandemic. As the aftermath of the pandemic unfolds and North American culture continues to evolve, perhaps faster than ever before, innovativeness is very likely to continue to be important in churches. This means that the elements of organizational culture that are necessary for innovation (creativity, organizational openness, future orientation, risk-taking, and proactiveness) need to be developed and prioritized (Hurley & Hult, 1998; Ruvio et al., 2014).

Creativity. In organizational contexts, creativity can be viewed as "the creation of a valuable, useful new product, service, idea, procedure, or process" (Woodman et al., 1993, p. 293) when people are working together to achieve goals defined by the organization's mission. During the pandemic, when traditional meetings were no longer possible, new ideas were needed for every type of ministry that contributed to a church's mission, ranging from children's ministry to evangelism, from weddings to funerals.

Some churches were equipped with very creative leaders who came up with many new ideas to respond to the needs. Less creative churches may have chosen to depend on the creativity of other churches and copy what they were doing; this strategy would have undoubtedly been superior to simply making a small number of not-especially creative changes so that the church could function by providing minimal services to its members. Leaders of churches that are members of active church networks (or denominations) were able to share and discuss creative ideas more easily than churches that are not members of such networks.

Organizational Openness. Innovation requires more than creative and useful ideas. The organization needs to be open to these ideas in order to implement them. This requires both adaptability, the ability to adjust programs in order to meet people's needs as the context changes, and flexibility, the willingness to replace existing programs with new ones more appropriate to the present context.

Organizations (e.g., churches) that are led by open-minded people tend to be higher in organizational openness than organizations with less open-minded leaders. People high in the personality trait of openness (one of the Big Five personality traits) tend to be curious, have a willingness to try new ideas, hold unconventional ideas, tolerate ambiguity, and are willing to consider views that differ from their own (DeYoung et al., 2005;

McCrae, 1996). Moreover, the structure of an organization also influences its openness. In churches with boards that require unanimity before new ideas can be implemented, any board member can block any change, reducing the organizational openness of the church to very low levels. On the other hand, churches where the head pastor or people responsible for specific ministries have the freedom to act as they see fit without seeking approval from others tend to have higher organizational openness. Nevertheless, churches with leaders who have little accountability are ripe for abuse, especially among leaders who are low in humility (Dunaetz, Jung, and Lambert, 2018; Puls, 2020).

Future Orientation. Another element of a church's culture that is essential for innovativeness is a focus on the future. It is all too easy for a church to be focused on what has worked in the past, a conservativism reinforced by evangelical theology which looks at Christ's death as the central point of human history. However, the centrality of Christ's death and resurrection does not mean that human cultures are always the same or that the means by which we communicate the gospel should always be the same; the content of the message is unchanging, but not the forms of communication that we use (Hesselgrave, 1989; Hiebert, 1987; Moreau, 2012).

This means that churches which are looking toward the future to understand how culture is evolving and which have a clear vision of what the church is trying to accomplish will be equipped to adopt the innovations necessary to fulfill the Great Commission in the evolving context. This requires unconventional, out-of-the-box thinking and is closely linked to both creativity and organizational openness.

Risk Taking. A willingness to commit resources to achieve long-term goals is the principal component of risk-taking (Ruvio et al., 2014). This can be expressed through the hiring of new staff people with specialties in technologies and strategies appropriate for the developing environment. But it can also simply mean modifying existing programs to see if the changes create improvements and undoing the changes if they do not. Like organizational openness, risk-taking without accountability can lead to major problems. Accountability means that one may be called to justify one's decisions and behaviors, with appropriate negative consequences if they cannot be justified (Lerner & Tetlock, 1999). A wise approach for accountability in a church is to have strong negative consequences for decisions and behaviors which violate moral principles, but much lighter (or even no) negative consequences for decisions and behaviors which fail to contribute to a church's mission but do not violate moral principles. This creates an atmosphere where experimenting with innovative ideas is safe.

Proactiveness. Rather than simply modifying or adding new programs to a church's ministry to better meet the needs of those influenced by the church, proactiveness requires looking for new opportunities in the external environment of the church and putting them into action. Similar to a missional approach to ministry (Guder, 1998; Stetzer, 2006; Van Rheenen, 2006), proactive churches need to be looking for new opportunities to bring the gospel to people who need it and help them become disciples of Jesus. During the pandemic, such innovations were especially driven by technology during the periods of lock-down.

When was Innovativeness the Most Important?

In this study, church size, member age, and member tenure did not moderate the relationship between church innovativeness and church commitment; the relationship was equally strong regardless of how these factors varied.

Church Size. Nevertheless, church size was positively correlated with both innovativeness and church commitment. Larger churches (compared to smaller churches) were viewed as more innovative. Several factors might account for this. Larger churches most likely have a history of success and innovation and are less likely to have a gate-keeping structure that resists innovation; they are likely to be higher in organizational openness to change than smaller churches. Moreover, they have the resources to be more innovative and to hire visionary leaders. The importance of this is seen during periods of crisis such as the pandemic. Since members of larger churches are more committed to their churches than members of smaller churches in this study, it appears that larger churches will come out of the pandemic stronger relative to smaller churches. This is an example of "the rich get richer and the poor get poorer" phenomenon that is often the case when technology-based changes are introduced into a context (Dunaetz et al., 2015; Kraut et al., 2002); those who are best equipped (in terms of ability and motivation) to implement a new technology successfully will benefit more from its introduction than those who are less equipped.

Gender. This study found that the relationship between perceived church innovation and church commitment is stronger for women than for men. Why would this be? Certainly, much new technology was introduced into church programs, especially video streaming of services and activities. In general, men are more receptive to technology and more interested in it (Tarafdar et al., 2011). However, the relationship between innovativeness and commitment was weaker in men than in women, indicating that something beyond technology was driving church commitment. Technology *per se* does not seem to be the driving force behind the relationship between perceived church innovativeness and church commitment. We should look toward other gender differences to explain this difference.

Women are more relationship-oriented than men, not in the sense that high-quality close relationships are more important to women than men, but in that social support and community integration are more important to women's psychological well-being than they are to men (Simon, 2002; Umberson et al., 1996). This may very well be the reason for the differences between men and women in the strength of the relationship between church innovativeness and church commitment.

Thus, it is quite possible that the relationship between church innovativeness and church commitment was stronger in women than in men during the pandemic because of women's greater appreciation for innovations which contributed to relationship maintenance and relationship development. This would mean that church commitment would be especially high when innovations were introduced that would enable them to maintain and develop their relationships with other church members; when these innovations were not present, commitment would be lower. This would explain why the relationship between church innovation and church commitment was stronger in women than in men.

Since much of what Christ calls Christians to do, such as loving one another (John 15:12), serving one another (Mark 10:42-45), and making disciples (Matt. 28:18-19), consists essentially of social activities, women's reactions to situations and innovations can provide a measure of how well the church is structured to be able to fulfill this calling. This stronger relationship between innovativeness and commitment in women than men may indicate that churches that provided relationship-oriented innovations more successfully helped people navigate the dangers of isolation and loneliness which threatened their well-being during the pandemic, enabling them to maintain and even develop relationships which are fundamental to the Christian life.

When unable to hold on-campus meetings, many churches introduced Zoom, Facebook livestreaming, or other online video-based apps into their programs. It is likely that some churches retained member commitment more effectively than others because they were able to move the main church activities where social interaction had previously occurred to an online context that maintained these social interactions. This means that churches where fellowship and social interaction occurred mainly in a large group context (such as after a worship service, as may be the case in a small church) would have a difficult time maintaining members if they simply started livestreaming worship services. However, in churches where fellowship and social interaction occurred primarily in small groups (as is typical in medium and large churches), successfully moving the small groups to a video chat platform would make maintaining and developing relationships more likely. Such innovations that maintain and develop relationships (rather than the programs) were likely to be the most important innovations that churches could introduce during the pandemic.

Limitations and Future Research

As is the case with all survey-based research, this study was correlational in nature rather than experimental, which means the direction of causation cannot be determined with certainty; it is possible that high church commitment causes a person to believe that his or her church is more innovative, rather than church innovativeness causing a person to increase in church commitment. However, in most churches, it is likely that the leadership is transparent enough and that the church members are sufficiently aware of the programs to understand where the church stands on the various dimensions of innovativeness. Further studies of church innovativeness, with innovativeness measured by outside, neutral observers, could provide additional evidence for the causal direction. Within individual churches, church leaders can run informal experiments by introducing elements of innovativeness into the church (new programs, vision casting, publicly valuing organizational openness, etc.) and note how people respond within the specific, local context. The introduction of new programs and technology which increase social interaction could also provide evidence for the importance of this type of innovation in a specific church's context.

Similarly, we cannot be sure that the results of this study would be the same in contexts other than that of the COVID-19 pandemic. Further studies in more normal contexts, especially looking at the connections between innovativeness, relationship maintenance and development, and church commitment can provide greater clarity.

Conclusion

This study has found evidence that innovativeness increased church commitment during the COVID-19 pandemic. It appears that the innovations that strengthened relationships might have been the most important during this period. It is quite possible that this phenomenon will continue to occur in churches after the pandemic. If this is the case, innovativeness will continue to be very important and church leaders should strive to increase it through vision casting, leadership selection, developing organizational openness, and especially through introducing new, creative programs and activities that create and solidify relationships between members.

References

Allen, N. J., & Meyer, J. P. (1990). The measurement and antecedents of affective, continuance and normative commitment to the organization. *Journal of Occupational Psychology, 63*(1), 1-18.

Barna, G. (1993). *Turn around churches: How to overcome barriers to growth and bring new life to an established church.* Regal Books.

Bothma, C. F., & Roodt, G. (2013). The validation of the turnover intention scale. *South African Journal of Human Resource Management, 11*(1), 1-12.

Caruana, A., Ewing, M. T., & Ramaseshan, B. (2002). Effects of some environmental challenges and centralization on the entrepreneurial orientation and performance of public sector entities. *Service Industries Journal, 22*(2), 43-58.

Choi, S., & Choi, J.-S. (2014). Dynamics of innovation in nonprofit organizations: The pathways from innovativeness to innovation outcome. *Human Service Organizations: Management, Leadership & Governance, 38*(4), 360-373.

Cronbach, L. J. (1951). Coefficient alpha and the internal structure of tests. *Psychometrika, 16*(3), 297-334.

Dess, G. G., Lumpkin, G. T., & Covin, J. G. (1997). Entrepreneurial strategy making and firm performance: Tests of contingency and configurational models. *Strategic Management Journal, 18*(9), 677-695.

DeYoung, C. G., Peterson, J. B., & Higgins, D. M. (2005). Sources of openness/intellect: Cognitive and neuropsychological correlates of the fifth factor of personality. *Journal of Personality, 73*, 825-858.

Dunaetz, D. R., & Bocock, J. (2020). Ministry involvement of church staff and volunteers: The role of organizational commitment and work engagement. *Theology of Leadership Journal, 3*(1), 52-67.

Dunaetz, D. R., Cullum, M., & Barron, E. (2018). Church size, pastoral humility, and member characteristics as predictors of church commitment. *Theology of Leadership Journal, 1*(2), 125-138.

Dunaetz, D. R., Jung, H. L., & Lambert, S. S. (2018). Do larger churches tolerate pastoral narcissism more than smaller churches? *Great Commission Research Journal, 10*(1), 69-89.

Dunaetz, D. R., Lisk, T. C., & Shin, M. (2015). Personality, gender, and age as predictors of media richness preference. *Advances in Multimedia, 2015*(243980), 1-9.

Dunaetz, D. R., Smyly, C., Fairley, C. M., & Heykoop, C. (2021). Values congruence and organizational commitment in churches: When do shared values matter? *Psychology of Religion and Spirituality*, Advance online publication.

Dykes, W. W. (2018). *Play well: Constructing creative confidence with LEGO® SERIOUS PLAY®*. Fielding Graduate University.

Ford, C. M. (2002). The futurity of decisions as a facilitator of organizational creativity and change. *Journal of Organizational Change Management, 15*(6), 635-646.

Garcia, R., & Calantone, R. (2002). A critical look at technological innovation typology and innovativeness terminology: A literature review. *Journal of Product Innovation Management, 19*(2), 110-132.

Gavetti, G., & Levinthal, D. (2000). Looking forward and looking backward: Cognitive and experiential search. *Administrative Science Quarterly, 45*(1), 113-137.

Guder, D. L. (Ed.). (1998). *Missional church: A vision for the sending of the church in North America*. William B. Eerdmans Publishing.

Hesselgrave, D. J. (1989). *Contextualization: Meanings, methods, and models*. Baker Book House.

Hiebert, P. G. (1987). Critical contextualization. *International Bulletin of Missionary Research, 11*(3), 104-112.

Hult, G. T. M., Hurley, R. F., & Knight, G. A. (2004). Innovativeness: Its antecedents and impact on business performance. *Industrial Marketing Management, 33*(5), 429-438.

Hurley, R. F., & Hult, G. T. M. (1998). Innovation, market orientation, and organizational learning: An integration and empirical examination. *Journal of Marketing, 62*(3), 42-54.

Hurley, R. F., Hult, G. T. M., & Knight, G. A. (2005). Innovativeness and capacity to innovate in a complexity of firm-level relationships: A response to Woodside (2004). *Industrial Marketing Management, 34*(3), 281-283.

Kelley, T., & Kelley, D. (2013). *Creative confidence: Unleashing the creative potential within us all*. Crown Publishing.

Kraut, R., Kiesler, S., Boneva, B., Cummings, J., Helgeson, V., & Crawford, A. (2002). Internet paradox revisited. *Journal of Social Issues, 58*(1), 49-74.

Lerner, J. S., & Tetlock, P. E. (1999). Accounting for the effects of accountability. *Psychological Bulletin, 125*(2), 255-275.

Lumpkin, G. T., & Dess, G. G. (1996). Clarifying the entrepreneurial orientation construct and linking it to performance. *Academy of Management Review, 21*(1), 135-172.

McCrae, R. R. (1996). Social consequences of experiential openness. *Psychological Bulletin, 120*, 323-337.

Meyer, J. P., & Allen, N. J. (1991). A three-component conceptualization of organizational commitment. *Human Resource Management Review, 1*, 61-89.

Miller, D., & Friesen, P. H. (1978). Archetypes of strategy formulation. *Management Science, 24*(9), 921-933.

Moreau, A. S. (2012). *Contextualization in world missions: Mapping and assessing evangelical models*. Kregel Publications.

Neighbour, R. W. (1973). *The seven last words of the church: Or "We never tried it that way before".* Zondervan Publishing House.

Penfold, G. E., & Taylor, G. L. (2020). *Restart churches: A proven strategy to restore vibrant ministry in your church.* ChurchSmart Resources.

Powell, R., Bellamy, J., Sterland, S., Jacka, K., Pepper, M., & Brady, M. (2012). *Enriching church life: A guide to results from National Church Life Surveys for local churches.* Mirrabooka Press & NCLS Research.

Powell, R., & Pepper, M. (2018). Local churches and innovativeness: An empirical study of 2800 Australian churches. *Research in the Social Scientific Study of Religion, 29,* 278-301.

Puls, D. (2020). Narcissistic pastors and the making of narcissistic churches. *Great Commission Research Journal, 12*(1), 67-92.

Rainer, T. S. (2020). *The post-quarantine church: Six urgent challenges and opportunities that will determine the future of your congregation.* Tyndale Momentum.

Rauch, A., Wiklund, J., Lumpkin, G. T., & Frese, M. (2009). Entrepreneurial orientation and business performance: An assessment of past research and suggestions for the future. *Entrepreneurship Theory and Practice, 33*(3), 761-787.

Ruvio, A. A., Shoham, A., Vigoda-Gadot, E., & Schwabsky, N. (2014). Organizational innovativeness: Construct development and cross-cultural validation. *Journal of Product Innovation Management, 31*(5), 1004-1022.

Salavou, H. (2004). The concept of innovativeness: Should we need to focus? *European Journal of Innovation Management, 7*(1), 33-44.

Simon, R. W. (2002). Revisiting the relationships among gender, marital status, and mental health. *American Journal of Sociology, 107*(4), 1065-1096.

Stetzer, E. (2006). The evolution of church growth, church health, and the missional church: An overview of the church growth movement from, and back to, its missional roots. *Journal of the American Society for Church Growth, 17*(1), 87-112.

Tarafdar, M., Tu, Q., Ragu-Nathan, T. S., & Ragu-Nathan, B. S. (2011). Crossing to the dark side: Examining creators, outcomes, and inhibitors of technostress. *Communications of the Association for Computing Machinery, 54*(9), 113-120.

Umberson, D., Chen, M. D., House, J. S., Hopkins, K., & Slaten, E. (1996). The effect of social relationships on psychological well-being: Are men and women really so different? *American Sociological Review, 61*(5), 837-857.

Van de Ven, A. H. (1986). Central problems in the management of innovation. *Management Science, 32*(5), 590-607.

Van Rheenen, G. (2006). Contrasting missional and church growth perspectives. *Restoration Quarterly, 48*(1), 25-32.

von der Ruhr, M., & Daniels, J. P. (2012). Examining megachurch growth: Free riding, fit, and faith. *International Journal of Social Economics, 39*(5), 357-372.

Wanberg, C. R., & Banas, J. T. (2000). Predictors and outcomes of openness to changes in a reorganizing workplace. *Journal of Applied Psychology, 85*(1), 132-142.

Wang, C. L., & Ahmed, P. K. (2004). The development and validation of the organisational innovativeness construct using confirmatory factor analysis. *European Journal of Innovation Management, 7*(4), 303-313.

Whitesel, B. (2020). *Growing the post-pandemic church*. ChurchLeadership.press.

Woodman, R. W., Sawyer, J. E., & Griffin, R. W. (1993). Toward a theory of organizational creativity. *Academy of Management Review, 18*(2), 293-321.

Appendix A: Church Innovativeness Scale

Adapted from Ruvio et al. (2013). The dimensions of innovativeness measured by each item are in parentheses. Participants indicate the level of their agreement with each of the statements.

1 = Strongly Disagree

2 = Disagree

3 = Neither Agree nor Disagree

4 = Agree

5 = Strongly Agree

1. My church is constantly looking to develop and offer new or improved ministries. *(Creativity)*

2. The leaders are encouraged to use original approaches when dealing with problems in church. *(Creativity)*

3. My church is open and responsive to change. *(Openness)*

4. The leaders in my church search for fresh, new ways of looking at problems. *(Openness)*

5. My church effectively ensures that the leaders and congregation share the same vision of the future. *(Future Orientation)*

6. My church likes to take big risks. *(Risk-Taking)*

7. My church does not like to "play it safe." *(Risk-Taking)*

8. The leaders are always seeking new opportunities for the church. *(Proactiveness)*

9. The leaders take the initiative in an effort to shape the environment to the church's advantage. *(Proactiveness)*

Appendix B: Church Commitment Scale

Based on Bothma & Roodt's (2013) Turnover Intention Scale 6 (TI-6) Participants indicate the level of their agreement with each of the statements.

> 1 = Strongly Disagree
> 2 = Disagree
> 3 = Neither Agree nor Disagree
> 4 = Agree
> 5 = Strongly Agree

1. I often look forward to going to church.
2. I often think about finding another church that will better suit my needs.*
3. I often consider leaving my church.*
4. My church very much satisfies my personal needs.
5. I am often frustrated in my church because my needs are not met.*
6. I would likely accept an invitation from another church to come visit it.*

Items marked with an asterisk (*) are reversed scored: 5 becomes 1, 4 becomes 2, etc.

About the Authors

Anna Covarrubias graduated with an M.S. in Organizational Psychology from Azusa Pacific University. Her passion is to equip Christian organizations to propel innovation and build healthy cultures.

David R. Dunaetz is Associate Professor of Leadership and Organizational Psychology at Azusa Pacific University, the editor of the *Great Commission Research Journal*, and formerly a church planter in France.

Wendi Dykes McGehee, PhD, is the Director of the Master of Science in Organizational Psychology at Azusa Pacific University. Her research portfolio centers around creative confidence, play, and innovation.

GREAT COMMISSION
RESEARCH JOURNAL
2021, Vol. 13(2) 71-104

SPECIAL SECTION

Innovations in Churches During the COVID-19 Pandemic

This section of the *Great Commission Research Journal* presents six case studies of innovations that were introduced into churches during the COVID-19 pandemic of 2020. Although pandemics have touched previous generations, many church leaders felt unprepared for the government regulations, the lockdowns, and the need to protect church members during what has become the deadliest pandemic of this generation.

The innovations described in these case studies represent some of the creative and effective ways that churches responded to the situation to continue focusing on the Great Commission. Some innovations should be kept and continue to be used after the pandemic is over. Others may serve as examples of what churches can do the next time a similar situation occurs. All six of these case studies are useful for comparing one's present church situation and pandemic response to what could have been done or to what can still be done and introduced into the church.

GREAT COMMISSION
RESEARCH JOURNAL
2021, Vol. 13(2) 73-76

The Quarantine Olympics of Cultivate Church in Athens, Alabama

Joel Franks

It was the best of times, then it was the worst of times. Dickens might have been writing that about 2020 for Cultivate Church in Athens, AL, outside of Huntsville. In January 2020, we celebrated our first anniversary as a church, achieved record highs for Sunday attendance (77), for mid-week Bible study attendance (45), and for the number of discipleship groups (7 groups). We were riding a wave of steady, solid growth. People were being saved and 7 had been baptized. A community of believers who cared for one another was being cemented together in the love of Christ. It was this feeling of community and family that was most attractive to people who came to visit almost every week.

Athens is a rapidly growing city with a population of 28,000 that is part of the Huntsville metropolitan area. Almost every person that joined our church community was from some other city or state. Not a single person in our church was native to Athens. As a result, the young church quickly came together as a group because these people did not have many relationships in town. Like the church's leadership team of 5 people, they had recently moved to Athens to take advantage of the booming development.

When our government imposed a stay-at-home order in April of 2020, my greatest fear was that we would lose that sense of togetherness. While it is quite possible to worship God through technology, there is no natural sense of community associated with using technology. Watching a screen is not the same as being physically in the same room as other believers.

There is nobody there to share a handshake or a warm hug after a rough week at work. There is no sanctuary from the trials that people deal with on a regular basis. In our church family, most everybody continued to work. So, the pressure of the daily grind was still there, but the release of that pressure that comes from fellowship with the family of God was gone.

As our leadership team met together, our focus was clear: How do we keep everybody engaged with each other while at the same time reaching out into the community to share the gospel? Obviously, we were going to have to think creatively. So, we bounced ideas off each other. Most of them were crazy and unfeasible. However, whenever many ideas are generated, there always seems to be one that grows into something useful.

My wife, Melanie, suggested a game show of some sort. I had never organized a game show. I don't watch game shows. I don't even like game shows! But as we brainstormed about the possibilities, we determined to give it a try. I knew that all successful church planters are willing to try new activities, activities that are different from what they have done in the past. Just because a church planter does not like an activity, it doesn't mean that it will be ineffective. Different is not a curse word. Different is not bad. Different may be difficult, but different is not bad when it has the potential to contribute to a church's God-ordained goals. It is true that church leaders might fail when they try something different, but why should that be a hindrance? Many times, we fail when we are doing the same old things we have done before, yet that doesn't stop us from doing the same old things! The Cultivate Church motto could have become "Never be afraid to try something different."

We decided to experiment with a gameshow to be broadcast on Facebook Live about two weeks after the lockdown started. The first event was a success, so for the two months that our community was under lockdown, we used Facebook Live to interact with the folks in our city as we played "Pictionary", "Family Feud", "Heads Up", and "Quarantine Survival Item Scavenger Hunt." We did our best to make it a Friday night must-see event. At our Sunday morning online services, we promoted this activity as the first-ever "Cultivate Quarantine Olympic Games." We created invitations to the games with a logo and a brief description. We encouraged the people of our church to share this invitation on their social media pages.

When that first Friday came, we wore "Quarantine Olympics" t-shirts and built a makeshift set in our home. I have found that you need hosts who are capable of being funny without trying too hard. My associate church planter and I are able to feed off each other's comments and improvise well. He plays the classic slapstick comedian to my straight character. We had a ball making the few members of our live audience (i.e., our families) laugh, knowing that the online viewers were enjoying it as well.

In order to achieve the goal of making contact with new families in Athens who weren't already familiar with our church, we created an invitation for an online scavenger hunt announcing a Quarantine Survival Package would be given as a prize to the winning household. We purchased a huge basket and filled it with all sorts of goodies for dad, mom, and the children. We included candies, snacks, books, and gift cards. We even added a few rolls of toilet paper when it was hard to come by! We promised that the winning family would receive contactless delivery to their home.

That Friday, we played a classic scavenger hunt. We would call out an ordinary household item that everyone would need to make it through an extended period at home. Each family had to find the item that was announced and text us a picture of themselves with that item. The first photo received earned a point. It was readily apparent that our families were having a blast as their pictures rolled in. Moreover, everybody got to see each other having fun as we shared the photos on Facebook Live. Most importantly, three new families that we had never met joined in on the fun, even sending us their photos to share with the others.

Before that first night was over, we had contacted several people that we did not know. Some of them joined us for online worship services the following Sunday. One family that first contacted us online during the lockdown now regularly attends our church. Fruit is still showing up from those "Quarantine Olympics" as I talked to a man just a few days ago that is watching our online services and plans to attend in person as soon as their new baby is able. He was one that I personally invited for a little fun on Friday nights during the stay-at-home-order.

As the restrictions lessened in our area, we began to do more in-person family events again, such as oil changes for single moms done by the men in the church with a brunch for these moms and their kids organized by the women in the church. But there is still a place for these online family fun times. When winter weather plagued the south in early 2021, many in our area were frightened to go out on the roads. So, we decided to run the gameshow again. Although we live in a culture that is saturated with media, this is something different from the norm. It is personalized. Even the small children that have notoriously short attention spans seem to stay engaged when they see a familiar face on the screen.

These online gameshows give our people something to invite their friends and family members to enjoy, many of whom do not attend church. We have another one planned in a few weeks. Cultivate was chosen as the name of the church with the idea of "Cultivating relationships with people as we all cultivate a relationship with Christ." These online events allow them to break the ice and cultivate relationships with others that lead to an opportunity to share the Gospel. Only then can they know what it is like to be a member of His family and become functioning members of the Cultivate family. Do not allow being stuck in the house to be an excuse to fail in evangelizing those who need to hear the gospel!

About the Author

Joel Franks is a husband to Melanie, father of Jonathan and Makayla, and a church planter with Free Will Baptist North American Ministries. He currently serves at Cultivate Church in Athens, Alabama.

CULTIVATE CHURCH
ATHENS, ALABAMA

Year founded: 2019
Denomination or Network: Freewill Baptist North American Ministries
Weekly Attendance: 70s
Location: suburban, 21 miles west of Huntsville

GREAT COMMISSION
RESEARCH JOURNAL
2021, Vol. 13(2) 77-84

Storytelling the Gospel in Hungary: Zooming in on an Ancient Mode of Communication

Keith Sellers

With the daily reminders of our mortality, during the pandemic my wife and I became energized to communicate the good news of Christ through dramatic storytelling. Michael Green (2004) tells us that the early Christians gave witness by using pericopes or short narratives from the life of Christ. The Medieval Church used mystery and miracle plays to reach and teach once illiterate European peoples. To enhance their presentations of Bible stories to Africans, Livingstone and other 19th century missionaries appropriated the 17th century Jesuit use of the "Magic Lantern," a device which included a fueled flame and mounted glass slides for projecting images (Simpson, 1997). Of course, storytelling is not just for children, the illiterate, or indigenous peoples! More than twenty years ago I dressed up as Pharaoh to help a Northern Virginia Baptist pastor talk about the Exodus story in an adult Bible class. This pastor planted a seed which years later bore fruit in another continent.

We serve in the Golgota 11 Church, a small, young church in the eleventh district of Budapest, as well as in summer day camp ministries held in a variety of venues across the Hungarian countryside. Reworking ancient storytelling with technology for the current crisis proved effective when we were limited to web-based meetings. The church suspended live services and met online from the third week of March 2020 until June 2020. As the pandemic waned during the summer months, we served in person at Christian day camps in small Hungarian towns. From summer until the end of October 2020, churches met in person, but when the third wave of the coronavirus hit hard, almost all churches closed their doors from November 2020 until late May 2021. When the world slowed down, we were able to rediscover and retool the ancient mode of storytelling the gospel both in summer day camps and with online children's meetings. Although we have contact with about 30 children in our church community, only three to ten kids met regularly for our online children's church meetings.

One of our ministries in Hungary involves communicating the gospel to unchurched kids from first to eighth grades at summer day camps, which are conducted much like a Vacation Bible School in the States. In the summer of 2020, we worked in five weeks of day camps in different towns across the Hungarian countryside in partnership with the Hungarian director of the Way of Hope Foundation in Hungary (http://www.wayofhope.co.uk). The Way of Hope Foundation seeks to evangelize families and youth as well as provide forms of social relief and educational opportunities like English or German language study camps. They usually serve disadvantaged communities in Hungary and Southwest Ukraine. Depending on the venue, the camp week saw anywhere from twenty-five to seventy-five kids. Two additional weeks of day camps were canceled due to the host school or town not wanting to risk the spread of the virus. The Hungarian government allowed smaller towns the choice of tightening or loosening restrictions depending on the weekly virus cases reported. Each day and every week we wondered whether any of us would fall victim to the virus and the entire week or remaining camps would be canceled. Thankfully every camp remained coronavirus-free.

As we pondered how to best present the gospel to young listeners, we concluded that we needed to do something that captures their attention. Unchurched kids certainly do not want to sit through an analytical lecture about the evidence for the Christian faith. Neither do I! Back in 2019 my wife first suggested the idea of using dramatic storytelling to engage kids at summer camps. My dressing up as a Bible character and having the character retell his encounter with Jesus is much more engaging than my typical lecture. Our rediscovered use of dramatic storytelling is certainly not original, but it proved especially handy during the pandemic year. We first used dramatic storytelling in the summer of 2019 with unchurched kids, and in 2020 we improved it for camp use. Also, whenever the government ordered restrictions on public gatherings, we used this approach online for our usual church kids. The government allowed churches which own their own buildings to meet during the pandemic, but churches like ours that rent their halls were not allowed to meet. Due to the severity of the third wave in Hungary, most churches closed their doors even if they owned their properties. Our church, Golgota 11, is affiliated with the Calvary Chapel movement in Hungary and is located in the eleventh district of Budapest. The church launched from the downtown mother church about nine years ago and fluctuates in total attendance from twenty to eighty. Just before the third wave of the pandemic hit in November, the church called a new pastor in late August of 2020.

To meet the need of constructively occupying children on summer break while their parents are at work, Hungarian churches and other ministries have for many years held day camp ministries available to the general public. Christian day camps attempt to meet a niche market such as helping youth improve second language proficiency or learning skills in a specific sport. Because we serve in Christian day camps to promote English language learning, we also seek to present the gospel in an effective way. The host, usually a church and sometimes a local mayor, informs parents of the inherently religious background of the camp program. Everyone knows ahead of time that the purposes are both academic and spiritual.

Contrary to what some may think, dramatic storytelling takes a lot more forethought and preparation than the typical lecture or sermon. The preparation involves not just lots of Bible study and prayer, but also reading history, gathering materials and costumes, preparing presentation slides for visual support, communicating with the hosting church or school, and continuous practice and revision of the script. Just before the pandemic intensified in the spring of 2020, I was spending winter back in Virginia visiting supporters in the Mid-Atlantic region. In early February I ordered some additional costumes and accessories, all made in China, shipped to the US, and then transported in my luggage to Budapest on March 2nd. While globalization may one day pose an ominous apocalyptic threat, it has never been so good for us in ministry! Hats off to Chinese manufacturing and Mr. Bezos for enhancing our efforts at evangelizing and teaching youth in Hungary! Those skilled in dressmaking could certainly have designed more authentic costumes, but the Amazon option was my lot as a missionary on the cheap and in a hurry to fly back to Europe. A recent addition to my wardrobe included a centurion costume as well as a selection of beards, a bald cap, a realistic-looking plastic chain, and other accessories to dress up as various key Bible characters (See Figure 1). From a wooden pole and metallic wood stain obtained at a German hardware chain store here in Budapest, I fashioned a satisfactory Roman javelin.

At some camps, I dressed up like the young Simon Peter who tells about one of his recent encounters with Jesus, whether on Lake Galilee or in the Garden of Gethsemane. His dialogue directly addresses the audience by conveying his incredulity of a miracle, his honest doubt, and his gradual process of coming to faith in the new rabbi from Nazareth. A fishing net and some rubbery plastic fish make for good props to throw at the audience to gain their immediate attention. At two other camps, I dressed up as various New Testament centurions, who told how they came to faith in Christ (Luke 7:1-10, Matt. 27:54, Acts 10:1-7). Pre-teen and adolescent young men, even the ones known for bad behavior, were especially attentive when the ancient soldier talked about his encounter with Jesus. Prior to the appearance of Peter or the centurion on stage, a youth or adult read the related gospel pericope in their heart language, and then the Bible character appeared speaking in English with a translator. The storyteller addressed the audience as if they were part of his ancient world. He assumed that they were traveling in an ancient caravan, which appeared to stop at Capernaum's Roman tax station or on the outskirts of Jerusalem during one of the Jewish festivals. The script integrated important details about the historical and geographical setting to enhance the listener's personal engagement with the biblical text and context. When playing Peter, I might point to an image of a first-century fishing boat if the venue has a projector. Peter described his fishing boat as a modern young man would enthusiastically speak about his new car. After the brief skit, I changed clothes and returned as myself to further explain the gospel story and its application to our lives in the present. In the middle of the week, I give my own testimony of how I came to faith as a young teen.

Of course, it would have been better to use two or three different people and more characters to enhance the depth of a scene, but as Jesus said, "the laborers are few," so we work with what we have. My only helpers were the translator, sometimes a young adult who read the related Scripture passage, and my wife who helped me dress up in the costume.

Before the summer began, I had to brush up on New Testament history, geography, and Roman centurions to knowledgeably portray the characters. Personal study on the New Testament centurions and Roman-era soldiers was enriching and helped me grasp the ancient quest for honor. Such background work is necessary in a European country which prides itself on historical parks and festivals held near ruins of Roman settlements (Scarbantia in modern Sopron, Aquincum in Budapest, and Sopianae in Pécs).

At the end of each week of camp, sometimes as early as on the third day, I asked the audience to consider making a decision to follow Christ. Almost every week at least one youth decided to follow Jesus. On the third day of a camp held in a public school, at least ten young people decided to follow Christ on hearing just three lessons about Peter's life. What is fascinating is that the use of dramatic storytelling does not require expert thespian ability nor Hollywood-style theatrical effects, but simply a storyteller who knows the story. At each day camp venue, I flexibly customized the props, lighting, and use of image projection. If image projection was not possible, I just compelled the audience to imagine the scene. Because we often served in economically depressed areas, a simple set posed no problems. Telling the story in an accurate, compelling way as well as boldly asking the audience to apply the story to their own lives are the most important tasks. Sometimes I took too much artistic liberty by not accurately portraying the biblical text, so I corrected myself in later presentations. Storytellers must continuously evaluate their performance to improve and communicate more effectively.

During the spring and fall months, my wife and I taught Sunday School in Hungarian from home via Zoom. Online attendance fluctuated from three to ten each Sunday. She typically asked someone to read a Bible passage online while I donned my costume in the garage. The dark, spider web filled garage with an ugly brown door provided a suitable backdrop on which to focus my iPad and utility light. When I portrayed Peter in prison, the ugly brown door fit the scene perfectly. At other times it fit the scene of nighttime or a dark room in a home. From another room, my wife integrated word games, live online interaction to review the story, and life application so that the children did not have merely a passive experience uncontextualized from their own lives. Sometimes we asked a couple of Hungarian college students to assist us online from their dormitory across town. They played word games and led the kids in action songs.

During one virtual Sunday School class, I dressed up as Peter in chains awaiting his death sentence in Rome. As an old man, he retold his encounters with Jesus when he was young, and how he often ended up in prison for the cause of Christ. The dismal-looking garage door nicely resembles the wall of a prison. Being under quarantine for so many weeks,

sort of a modern house-arrest, helped the listeners and the presenters better feel the isolation that Peter must have experienced. Another time I dressed up with long hair as the young John, and another time as the centurion at the cross. On Sunday, December 6th (the day when St. Nicholas delivers presents and candy to well-behaved children), my Deutsche Amazon-ordered St. Nicholas costume proved handy for posing as the beloved bishop of Myra. Nick told the kids about the original Christmas story and read from the Gospel of Luke. A donkey puppet and some olive oil helped us make a brief video to explain the meaning of Messiah, "the Anointed One."

On the Sunday just before Christmas, I dressed up as an old shepherd who reminisced about the night when angels appeared and how the Messiah was born in his small village. Sometimes I prerecorded the storytelling, especially since my memory of the Hungarian script is sometimes limited. Whether live or prerecorded, we taped pages of the script in large font to an old step ladder for an improvised teleprompter. Using Apple's free iMovie software on a six-year-old MacBook proved handy in editing my numerous mistakes and pauses to make the video flow better for attention-challenged kids. Watching humorous YouTube videos produced by other amateurs provided creative hints and ideas for our storyboards. The magic lantern has come a long way from Livingstone's day!

Storytelling holds several advantages for teaching the story of Christ's life, death, and resurrection. The pandemic prodded us to step back in time and diverge from the worn-out analytical gospel presentations of modernity. Because we have the advantages of both the ancient and the modern, we can hybridize storytelling with digital technology by using prerecorded video, slides, and live online presentation. By retelling short biblical narratives, the listener becomes automatically engaged. With storytelling, one does not have to defend each detail about the event because the storyteller gives his eyewitness account during which the listener tends to give the witness the benefit of the doubt. The skeptical heart is more easily disarmed and may even want to learn more. When playing the role of Peter or a shepherd, one does not have to portray himself as an educated and erudite apologist. Additionally, the veracity of the account is verified by the love and Christlike character of those explaining the application that immediately follows the story. The children know us, trust us, and still have a general respect for Jesus even when they do not understand what he is about. My stuttering and forgetfulness added to the scene of a simple person telling his story. The power of the Spirit who illuminates the redemptive story in the minds of the listeners made up for any thespian deficiencies in the storyteller. I've never had an acting class nor starred in a high school drama, but I know that we have a story that must be told.

Of course, a time will come when we need to modify this approach and innovate once again. As the world stood still, we took a step back to use an old method. By stepping backward, we were able to make a few big leaps forward for the Kingdom of Christ. Our churched kids enjoyed learning more about the Bible and did not seem the least bit bored. At the end of each summer camp week, I asked children and teens to consider becoming a Christ-follower. During the summer of 2020, at least twenty children raised their hands to indicate their decision to follow Christ. Because most people are reserved and very discrete about personal matters, we believe that the message likely affected more than the number of raised hands indicated.

References

Green, M. (2004) *Evangelism in the Early Church*, rev ed. Eerdmans Publishing.

Simpson, D. (1997) Missions and the Magic Lantern. *International Bulletin of Missionary Research, 21*(1), pp. 13-15.

GOLGOTA 11 CHURCH
BUDAPEST, HUNGARY

Year founded: 2012
Denomination or Network: Calvary Chapel
Weekly Attendance: 20s to 60s
Location: Urban, 4 miles south of the Parliament

About the Author

Keith Sellers and his wife Beverly have served in Hungary with WorldVenture Mission since 2000. Keith holds a D. Min. in Growing and Multiplying Churches from Talbot School of Theology, La Mirada, CA. They tell about their ministry experiences on their website at www.keithnbeverly.com.

GREAT COMMISSION

RESEARCH JOURNAL

2021, Vol. 13(2) 85-88

Digital Monastic Communities at Sumter Chapel, Americus, Georgia

Drew Anderson

In October 2019, we launched a new church, Sumter Chapel, here in Americus, a small town in South Georgia, with a core group of 30 people. Five months later, when we had grown to about 50, the pandemic hit our area. We had achieved all the numeric goals that were set and that could be expected of a new church in an area like ours. God had managed to gather people from different ethnicities, different socioeconomic classes, families and singles, old and young. But then we were suddenly scattered.

Before people could even truly connect.

Before the church had really even formed.

Before we even could get small groups and shared leadership in place. So, we did what everyone else did – pivoted. But we knew our pivot would not look like many churches, mostly because, when we started out, we were already not a typical church model. We had inherited an older church building but rearranged it to be able to sit around tables for conversation on Sunday mornings. We responded at prayer stations, including the Lord's Table. We preferred simplicity in our gathering and authentic relationships over produced worship settings. Our pivot had to match that reality. And we had to use technology to do so because of the stay-at-home order.

We immediately started an Examen prayer time on Facebook Live. Between 15 and 30 people attended each night for about 30 minutes. I posed reflection questions and people responded by posting comments that I would read aloud. That grew into starting an Instagram Live version as well, led by someone else on our team. These times allowed people to reflect upon their day, their emotions, where God was in the midst of it all, and what they were looking toward on the following day. It was uniquely powerful how connected we became.

Then we realized there could be more. This daily connection – the daily fellowship of the believers like we read about in Acts 2 could be accomplished via technology – if we simply leaned into it. We have since then been encouraging people to use any app they could to create these sorts of daily connections with one another – Facebook Messenger, WhatsApp, Marco Polo, Google Duo (soon we will be creating our own app). We quickly realized that the greatest hurdle for the church during this season was not how to offer an online weekly gathering, but to connect people on a daily basis to each other to share what God has been doing in their life.

This has become one of our main focuses in a way we never expected. Our desire is to maintain and create small "digital monastic communities" that meet both via technology and in-person. Presently we have started three of these communities with 8-25 members and hope to create another three this year. Because our culture is different than Rome in the 100s and 200s, it is not likely that we can completely recreate an Acts 2 experience; the ability to gather in-person every day in some way, especially for meals, would require communal living that would disrupt most people's lives. The only way to do that would be for people to move to a monastery or an intentional living community – but most would not be able to or want to do so. Even moving into the same neighborhood would not change the incompatibility of people's schedules and the difficulty of daily gatherings.

Therefore, we have been using technology to connect to one another in a consistent daily faith community – like a traditional monastic community. We then have weekly gatherings to physically connect with those same people. The leaders of our digital monastic communities all prefer smaller weekly gatherings, similar to Micro Churches or Missional Communities, over what people typically think of as church. We (the leaders of these communities) have started a network of these smaller gatherings during this year, one of the members of which is not connected to Sumter Chapel. So then, the people I see each week on Sunday at the church building, I also see or interact with every day on my phone. And then the third level of gathering we are creating is seasonal – based upon the Christian calendar and similar to the Jewish festivals. These will be times of larger gatherings for all the communities of the network which may be for celebrations, missional efforts, or other purposes. We will designate 3-4 times a year as the times that we bring together all those connected daily on the network's app and weekly in-person small groups in order to celebrate on a large scale what God is doing!

None of this was in the original vision God gave us.

None of it is a carbon copy of another ministry.

We have simply navigated this season and watched the ways God was already at work speaking to people and working in people's lives. Then we reflected upon how that might not merely be a short-term solution to get through the pandemic but might actually be God shifting our church "just in time." And when I say, "just in time," it's because we were already seeing the ineffectiveness of the current models to meet the next generation where they are. Most of Generation Z are digital natives, meaning they "live" online just as much as they live in-person. The digital world and the physical world are connected to them. So why would the church not meet them there?

Initially the idea of a daily digital community came out of my own personal experience using the app Marco Polo with a few friends. At the beginning of the quarantine, one of them suggested the three of us use the app for a group video chat. Two of us had never used it, but one had. And so, we tried it.

What proceeded for the next eight months was the formation of deep friendships formed in the context of sharing about our relationships with God simply thru leaving video messages for each other each day (sometimes multiple times a day, sometimes going days in-between). But the consistency of that video chat relationship, based in our collective relationship with God, has been transformative. The depth of our friendship, but also the depth of our relationships with God has been amazing. And it also provided us a space to process what we were going through together, to share deeply what was going on in our lives, to discern the direction God has wanted us to go, and to pray for one another about important things.

The three of us had only known each other for a month and spent about four days together at a conference right before COVID hit. We did not expect that a daily video chat app would take a brand-new friendship and turn it into a discipleship group. And yet it did, and we had not even restarted the in-person meetings weekly, nor had we started the seasonal gatherings.

So, we are expectant that God can do the same thing in more of these communities, that he can take small groups of people and use daily interaction through digital means to create deep faith communities – like we typically see in monastic settings – but do it in people's lives as they continue living where and how they already are.

Digital monastic missionaries is what we envision: members of digital monastic communities who are living fully present as missionaries in their everyday life – with their families, in schools, workplaces, neighborhoods, and communities.

We believe this can provide a way forward for the church that goes beyond simply maintaining the status quo. It calls us back to deep relationships with one another and with the God we read about in Acts.

We believe that this can be a needed reformation of the church – members who are no longer dependent on the weekly in-person large gathering but rather upon a daily walk with Jesus in the company of others.

We believe that God can use this to pour out His Spirit in fresh and new ways upon His people, to encourage people to live boldly where they are because of the support they are receiving, and to bring His Kingdom to our 21st century world using technology.

We believe the networks of digital natives today are roughly equivalent to the Roman roads upon which the message of the Gospel spread in Acts. So maybe the Church today, by embracing these modern Roman roads, can at least partially recover what was true of the Church in Acts – deep, transformative, world-changing faith communities.

About the Author

Drew and his wife, Sarah, and their two sons, currently live in Americus, GA, where Drew leads a new faith community named Sumter Chapel. In the last 5 years, they've helped to start a multiethnic fresh expression of church and are equipping others to start small expressions of church across South Georgia and beyond.

SUMTER CHAPEL
AMERICUS, GEORGIA

Year founded: 2019
Denomination or Network: Wesleyan Church
Weekly Attendance: 50
Location: Suburban, 2.5 hours south of Atlanta
Website: Sumterchapel.com

GREAT COMMISSION
RESEARCH JOURNAL
2021, Vol. 13(2) 89-93

Making Online Children's Ministry Interactive in Wheaton, Illinois

Eric Norregaard

Ping Ng

The children's ministry at Wheaton Chinese Alliance Church (Wheaton, Illinois) needed to move online during the pandemic, but we didn't want television for kids; we wanted to increase interaction between teachers, children, and parents. Rather than broadcasting a standard worship service as a predominately one-way form of communication, we developed an approach which is online yet interactive.

We knew our traditional approach to Sunday school and worship with about 35 children would have to change when we moved online. Having a Zoom children's Sunday school back-to-back with a Zoom children's worship on the same day would simply be too long for children to endure. And even if they could endure it, it would still be mostly one-way communication. So we took our "Sunday School" and moved it to midweek while keeping an online children's worship service late Sunday afternoon where the Sunday School material is reviewed. And we structured it in such a way as to foster interaction.

Each week we prepare a Google Slides file containing what we call an eBible lesson. The Google Slides file includes a creative presentation of the Bible passage, sandwiched by embedded videos of one of our teachers introducing and then explaining the central meaning of the passage. All of this is crucial because we believe we need to do our creative best to clearly communicate God's Word, just as Jesus used creativity, parables, and metaphors when he spoke. But Jesus did more than that; he fostered interaction, he asked questions, he asked his disciples what they thought. And from this angle, probably the most important part of the packet in terms of fostering interaction is the included homework questions for the children to complete along with their parents. The goal here is to draw the children out. Usually, there are three questions along with one or two challenge questions for the older children. We strive to create questions that do not have simple factual answers but that elicit thought and emotion such as "What do you think Jesus wants to clean up in your heart and in the world?" One of the questions always asks the child to draw some part of the Bible story. Because the children are at home and not in a classroom, they have as much time as they want to complete the assignment. We ask the parents to help the children complete the homework, take a picture of the completed assignment and email it to us. We don't grade their homework and we don't glance at it and file it away, but more of what we do with it later.

The "eBible lesson" is sent to parents' email addresses and provides flexibility for the parents and children to finish the lesson on their own at their convenience. The lesson is in the form of a Google Slides file. We have been using Brite Awana as our basic curriculum as we find that it has enough material for our teachers to design their own lessons.

Then on Sunday, we have a 4:30-5:30pm children's service on Zoom, using gallery view so the 15-20 children and 8-10 teachers can see each other. Unlike the traditional in-person worship, the children in their home environment are more relaxed as they participate in prayer, sing with muted audio, and respond to questions in the large group. One child will lead the opening prayer. Another child and his or her family will lead the singing. The children's service teacher will show the same creative video presentation of the Bible passage that the children watched at midweek. There are six-minute, age-divided breakout rooms with about 6 children per room, led by the teachers. The questions in the breakout room usually include some of the questions given in the homework assignment in the eBible lesson. The children are encouraged to verbally share their answers to questions they have already answered in their written homework. Because they have had time to process these questions at midweek, they don't feel put on the spot in their breakout rooms and can voice what they've previously written.

At the end, all the completed homework assignments that the parents have sent us will be shared with everyone on Zoom via Google Slides. The eBible lesson teacher will acknowledge each child's effort through words of encouragement. As the homework usually asks the children to draw some part of the Bible story, and as we can tell that the children usually spend significant time working on their drawings, we find that it's important to look for the details expressed in the picture and notice the insights the student revealed. Since we have strived to create open-ended homework questions that elicit the child's thoughts and emotions, and since the midweek setting has given them time and space to process and reflect on their answer, it's very important that we take time to pay attention to what they have written or drawn. Our goal is not to evaluate them, but to notice them. By taking time to appreciate the students' work, they realize that their work, feelings, and thoughts are being treated with respect. This incentivizes them to also do the next week's assignment as they know that their work will be appreciated. Oftentimes, this homework review segment becomes an additional teachable moment as the teacher finds the opportunity to bring up the main point of the lesson while commenting on the homework, but now the point is in direct connection to something the student has shared, so it is more powerful.

Essentially, we are - at midweek - doing our creative best to communicate God's Word and its application to their lives, then asking them to do their creative best to express their thoughts and feelings regarding God's presence in their lives. Then that bridges to Sunday when we pay attention to what they have expressed and give them encouragement. This is how we attempt to overcome the impersonal nature of the online world and foster interaction.

In making our online children's ministry interactive, we have had to respond to the needs and considerations of our unique situation. We found that parents with more than one child were unwilling to do more than one eBible lesson midweek. So, we merged five grade-specific classes into one online class in which all children from kindergarten through 5th grade were combined. So, the parent with two or three children may need to help all of them, but they are all working on the same lesson, thus making it easier on the parents.

One major challenge with having children of many abilities and maturity levels grouped together is the lack of individual attention possible; some children may be lost while others might be bored. Breakout rooms grouped according to age, and the attention given to each child's homework are two ways we have tried to address this challenge. For some of the older children who are tempted to withdraw and turn off their cameras, we have found it helpful to give them the responsibility to lead some part of the Sunday service. Again, we try to foster involvement to counter a tendency to self-isolate.

The online format is completely dependent on parental cooperation. The children in our region do not have email addresses or cell phones or social networks through which we can reach them. All communication has to go through the parents, and parental involvement is necessary to help the children complete their assignments and send in their work. We have lost some children because there are parents who find this to be too much trouble.

At the same time, we have also gained new families and children as our members have told friends, even some out of state, about this ministry available to their children. Through making our online children's ministry interactive, we have been able to find ways to lead the children in worship, teach them God's Word, and respectfully listen to them as they share with us their own understanding of God and His connection to their lives.

This online and interactive approach is even more demanding than our previous approach. Not only does it require more time in preparation, but it requires more buy-in and time investment by parents. In our traditional approach, a parent needed only to drop off their child for us to teach. Now it requires their involvement to help their child learn what we are teaching. And it requires regular encouragement by phone or email from us to the parents to stay involved. This however is an opportunity for us to increase our interaction with families, for parents to be more involved in the spiritual development of their own children, and for the parents to see themselves as coworkers in the ministry of the Gospel.

Online children's ministry doesn't have to be impersonal. No, we cannot give hugs. But we can still learn to notice the children, draw out their thoughts and feelings, and listen carefully. Many children lack someone who is really willing to listen to them. We can learn to do that, even online. We can make online children's ministry interactive.

WHEATON CHINESE ALLIANCE CHURCH
WHEATON, ILLINOIS

Year founded: 1978
Denomination or Network: Christian and Missionary Alliance
Languages Used in Worship: English, Mandarin, Cantonese
Weekly Attendance: (2019) 262
Location: Suburban, 25 miles west of Chicago
Website: wcac-cma.org

About the Authors

Ping Ng has served the children in Wheaton Chinese Alliance Church for 35 years as a teacher and for the last eight years as chair of the children's ministry.

Eric Norregaard served in Wheaton Chinese Alliance Church's youth ministry for 14 years and is now a teacher in the children's ministry.

GREAT COMMISSION
RESEARCH JOURNAL
2021, Vol. 13(2) 95-100

Quick Responses to Community Needs in Two Churches During the Pandemic

Brad Ransom and Edward Moody

Many churches have been doing the same thing for decades to reach people with the Gospel. The pandemic in the early spring of 2020 shook most churches to the core. Cities, counties, and states in the US began issuing stay-at-home orders. Churches across the country (and the world) were forced to stop gathering in person. Almost overnight, our methods for reaching people were invalid. No longer could the "come and see" or "seeker service" be used to introduce people to the Gospel or to our churches. Many churches adapted quickly while others moved more slowly. Only time will tell, but it appears that the churches which made quick changes navigated the rough seas easier than those which were slow to adapt.

Many churches with congregational rule in the US have a complicated structure which includes committees that must grant their approval and eventually a vote by the body in order to make changes to a church's meeting schedule, ministries, and philosophical approach. Some are slow to implement the changes which must be approved by a long process. During the 2020 pandemic, there simply was not time for many of these churches to move through their normal procedures, and they were forced to either break tradition or move very slowly in the quickly changing climate of the "pandemic church."

In this article, we will look at two churches that adapted quickly and rebounded in places where the restrictions were among the tightest in the country. They adapted by changing the way they utilized technology and ministered to the community.

Two Very Different Churches: The Bridge and Bluepoint

The Bridge Church in Fredericksburg, Virginia, launched March 1, 2020, with 227 people in a local public-school gymnasium. The Bridge Church is part of the National Association of Free Will Baptists. Suburban Fredericksburg (population 24,000) is about 1 hour and 30 minutes south of Washington, DC. On March 30, 2020, a stay-at-home order was issued, just weeks after the launch of the church.

On the other hand, Bluepoint Church is in Cisne, Illinois, a rural town with a population of 672, two hours east of St. Louis, MO, and three hours west of Louisville, KY. Bluepoint Church is 123 years old with a senior pastor who has served for 36 years and like the Bridge, is part of the National Association of Free Will Baptists. Both churches adapted quickly to the pandemic.

The Bridge Church

The Bridge Church was led by lead church planter, Chris Davenport. He learned to lead an infant congregation during a global pandemic on the fly.

The Bridge Church quickly shifted from Sunday morning services to daily connections with their community. The church immediately launched several house church gatherings (limited in size by State directives) which continued to meet weekly throughout the church shutdown period. In each of these gatherings, the focus was outreach and discipleship. They adapted and promoted the "M" model of discipleship originally developed by Stadia (stadiachurchplanting.org).

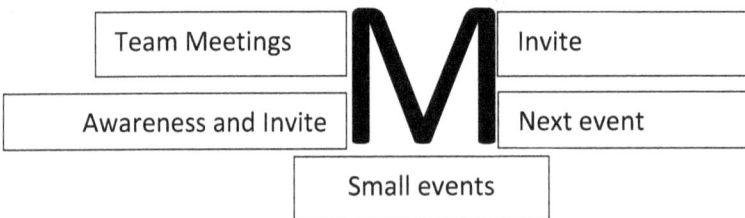

The lower left leg of the M represents awareness of people's needs and invitations to the church where these needs can be met. The top left peak on the M stands for meetings of teams of people who sought to support one another through fellowship and create programs to meet the community's needs. The bottom middle point focuses on small events that they could do for their neighbors, coworkers, and community within the stay-at-home guidelines, such as small group Bible studies or writing letters to express appreciation to frontline workers; at first most of these events were held online, and then as the restrictions were lowered, in small groups of two or three families. The top right peak of the M encourages church members to constantly invite others outside of the church to the church (small group) gatherings. The lower right point connects people to the next church-sponsored event. Everyone was encouraged to think through this model and implement it in their daily personal lives.

In addition, every person connected with the church was encouraged to create a "FAN" list. "FAN" is an acrostic for "Friends, Associates, and Neighbors." As each person developed a list of their unchurched friends, associates, and neighbors, they were coached on how to move them through the M model of discipleship.

Another innovation was the use of video technology. The church was blessed to have a professional filmmaker and videographer on their team who immediately went to work shooting and producing not only Sunday sermon videos but also promotional and encouraging videos addressed to the town of Fredericksburg as a community.

Writing Ministry. The Bridge Church began a letter-writing ministry and hand-wrote over 1,000 letters and cards to nurses and teachers. They were able to get other churches involved as well. The wife of one of the pastors was a nurse in the community hospital who was able to deliver them to other nurses. It was not unusual to find Pastor Davenport's business card at the nurse's station at the hospital, and the church received many contacts through the writing ministry.

Food Ministry. Since many of the students in the area received their food from the schools they attended, it became critical to distribute food. The Bridge Church, which was renting a public school for their Sunday meetings, used the relationships they had developed to partner with the city's schools to supply food for families. They also partnered with government agencies and restaurants using a "drop off" system which included delivering gift cards to families from restaurants as well as sealed and packaged meals from restaurants. This became a ministry to the restaurants which desperately needed the revenue; the church provided volunteers and drivers who would order food from local restaurants, pick it up and deliver it.

The church also sought to minister to other frontline workers. Many of the teachers were discouraged, so the church endeavored to bless them with gift cards. The church also partnered with restaurants to provide barbeque and donuts to law enforcement officers during the social justice protests that took place in the summer.

Bluepoint Church

When the governor of Illinois issued a stay-at-home order on Saturday, March 21, 2020, Pastor Ernie Lewis began posting a prerecorded daily morning devotion on Facebook. The church had not been using its website, so they redoubled their efforts to update it. They worked with their worship team and began recording and broadcasting services to post on Facebook and their website. The church was surprised by how many people watched their services and especially by the response from people in other towns in the county who contacted them about their services.

There was nothing technologically excellent about the broadcasts. For example, after a glitch, the first service was broadcast rotated 90 degrees. However, the key was consistency and steady improvement with an encouraging tone.

Many of the elderly became isolated in the community. The isolation was exacerbated by their limited technological skills with smartphones that most of the elderly had received from their children. To address this, during pastoral visits to the elderly, the pastor would ask to add a shortcut icon to their phones which took them directly to the church's live stream.

Writing Ministry. Bluepoint Church wanted to keep in contact with its members. The church leaders did so by writing weekly letters and sending cards to congregants on holidays. Additionally, the community has a newspaper which is widely read by the elderly in the community. The church submitted a weekly article to keep the community updated about activities and resources the church was providing (e.g., food distribution and devotions).

Food Ministry. The Bluepoint Church also worked with local government officials to provide watermelons and cantaloupes for people in the community. As a small community, the church and government officials were well acquainted with each other. The church also received boxes of groceries that members were able to distribute to people who had been identified to be in need. In addition to responding to physical needs, this distribution provided emotional support to those who had been isolated. One parishioner had just opened a restaurant before the onset of COVID. The church bought meals for people in the community from this restaurant, so they were able to meet the needs of others as well as support the local restaurant. Church leaders were able to interact with the people when they dropped the food off. Often long discussions ensued in the yard of the recipients.

Providing Encouragement. Indoor funeral services were not a possibility, but Bluepoint began conducting outdoor funeral services that were allowed for families. These funerals, and food prepared by the church, provided support and encouragement to the families who lost loved ones during this dark time.

Building Renovation. Before COVID, the Bluepoint Church had planned to remodel its building. Since they were unable to conduct services, this worked to their advantage. It was easier to conduct the renovation, and it provided an opportunity to feel a sense of community. Since only the contractors were allowed on the premises for the work, church leaders made a photo album to document the progress and included pictures of various church members to the degree possible. As meals were delivered to the community, people would look at the photo album. Though isolated, seeing the building progress and photos of church members made them feel that they were part of something bigger.

Adapting Quickly Led to Critical Results

The Bridge Church recently celebrated its one-year anniversary and was able to meet in person. In their short history, they have had eight confessions of faith, eight baptisms, and 17 rededications. They have made an indelible impact on the community of Fredericksburg, Virginia. While they saw an average of 70 online viewers each week during the shutdown period, they have averaged almost 78 in weekly attendance since they have been allowed to resume services in person. Although a one-year-old church averaging just under 80 is not record-breaking, the Bridge Church is a church that has greatly impacted its community. It has continued to use its home church groups as community small groups and is planning to add new groups soon. Ask anyone in town, and they will likely identify The Bridge as a church that cares about people and the community.

Though Bluepoint Church is in an entirely different context, they, too, were able to have a positive impact on their community. As Pastor Lewis noted, "You just have to adapt and do what you can." The leaders of the church became convinced they could not go back to ministry as it was before the pandemic.

Both churches have noted that they made contacts in the pandemic they would never have made otherwise. Sometimes this was through their technology, but other times it was through their partnerships with community leaders. Many people's eternity depends on the local church in their community; we all need to be innovators as we navigate our churches' futures in a post-pandemic age.

About the Authors

Brad Ransom is a native of Southern California but spent 33 years of his adult life serving churches and his denomination in Oklahoma. He currently serves as Director of Church Planting and Chief Training Officer for Free Will Baptist North American Ministries in Nashville, Tennessee. His passion is training and coaching pastors to plant and revitalize churches. Ransom currently serves as the first Vice President of the Great Commission Research Network.

Edward E. Moody, Jr. serves as the executive secretary of the National Association of Free Will Baptists. He served as pastor at Tippett's Chapel in Clayton, North Carolina, for almost two decades. He is a former associate dean and professor at the school of education at North Carolina Central University.

BLUEPOINT CHURCH
CISNE, ILLINOIS

Year founded: 1898
Denomination or Network: National Association of Freewill Baptists
Weekly Attendance: 130
Location: Rural, two hours east of St. Louis, MO
Website: bluepointchurch.com

THE BRIDGE CHURCH
FREDERICKSBURG, VIRGINIA

Year founded: 2020
Denomination or Network: National Association of Freewill Baptists
Weekly Attendance: 80
Location: Suburban, an hour and a half south of Washington, DC
Website: bridgefbg.com

GREAT COMMISSION
RESEARCH JOURNAL
2021, Vol. 13(2) 101-104

Innovations in a Nursing Home Ministry

H. L. Ward, Jr.

When I think of innovation, the first person who comes to mind is the fictional character, Angus "Mac" MacGyver, the star of a hit television series that was first introduced in 1985 and later rebooted in 2016. Special Agent MacGyver was quite adept at getting out of a jam using his genius intellect, a Swiss Army knife, and any basic items available in his immediate vicinity. He never seemed to panic and always kept focus, which allowed him to come out on top of any situation without resorting to violence or use of deadly force. MacGyver was an innovator and was always capable of adapting to changes without succumbing to distress. As a result, he preserved his life and those whom he was entrusted to save.

Innovation is the buzzword for responding to the multi-faceted challenges presented by the pandemic. Over the past year, I have found myself navigating the "new normal" in ministry practices amidst the restrictions placed upon our evangelistic outreach to the local nursing homes here in northwest Florida. Before I explain the particular innovation we implemented, I would like to give you some background information.

Approximately five years ago, I was led to start a ukulele group that would rehearse weekly with the intent to perform monthly at our area nursing home. Although we played sacred and secular tunes, I would always weave the Gospel into every performance. Unlike any other form of treatment, music awakens the spirit of those held physically and mentally captive through dementia, Alzheimer's or Parkinson's diseases. Several members of our congregation were on the senior living side of the residence, but many had moved over to memory care due to these illnesses. We felt those in the nursing home were often overlooked and forgotten – their memory truly lost. We were faithful to honor the Lord's calling to go and share His love and truth through music to them – no matter how much time they had left with us. As we sang the familiar hymns, I could see those lips move and sing with us. Their faces lit up and their eyes twinkled. Even the residents that were not necessarily connected with a church felt the Spirit of God move through His Word and power. It was awesome to behold, and over the course of the next several years, our musical outreach ministry gained momentum exponentially. In the course of a year, we added an additional group of ukulele players comprised of third through eighth graders. They were assigned to another local nursing home. Over the course of four years, these groups rehearsed weekly and performed monthly as part of an evangelistic outreach ministry of Community Church. During the summer months the groups would combine in their efforts and facilitated an environment where five generations could interact and serve the community.

In March of 2020, everything came to a grinding halt. We were restricted from entering any of the facilities because of the COVID pandemic. Initially, we were also restricted from rehearsing in person. The ministry doors into the nursing homes were literally closed. We all desired to find a way to stay connected and polished in our skills. It took some creative thinking, prayer, and persistence, but thanks to current communications technology, we were able to redeem the situation. I utilized a Zoom meeting setup to keep everyone together and informed on our next steps. I began praying for wisdom to know how I could still minister to those disconnected from our merry band of ukulele players. Zoom meetings provided such a great opportunity to keep everyone engaged through online rehearsals and discussion on evangelistic outreach continuing through the pandemic. This facilitated connection among the group and communication with the leadership for the area nursing homes.

Over the next two months, I began reaching out to the facilities to see what creative avenues we might consider to safely connect and encourage the residents. While the age group at the nursing homes was considered at-risk for COVID, I knew the emotional impact of isolation was another huge risk factor. I began to proactively reach out to leadership and regional directors to express these concerns and seek solutions, even inviting them on our Zoom meeting calls with ukulele players. It was important for all involved to see the impact of our ministry—not to mention the strength in sheer numbers committed to seeing it through into this "new normal." We were able to convey the importance of the emotional well-being of the residents and assure leadership that we might have to figure out a way to minister—even if it meant digitally or isolated in a small area outside. Prayer and persistence in this endeavor paid off in the long run.

Since many of the large, assisted living facilities are corporately owned, they maintain a corporate mentality to protect assets and liabilities. The legal ramifications associated with the coronavirus seemed to overshadow everything to the point that the emotional risk factors of isolation had not been adequately taken into consideration. This fact was fully realized when one of my church members in the memory care facility passed away. I ended up working with one of her local family members to plan the funeral via live stream, because no out-of-state family members were allowed to attend—just one of the daughters, a son-in-law, and the father who just lost his wife of nearly 74 years. It was heartbreaking for both the surviving husband and the family who was only allowed to see the funeral via live stream. Once the funeral was over, the widower went back to assisted living and remained in quarantine for two weeks. Less than one month later, this saddened and lonely husband passed. I believe it was a combination of grief at the loss of his wife of so many years and also the fact that he remained in isolation from his support and encouragement.

After several discussions concerning the greater risk factors of isolation, we were allowed to begin performing outside the facility with limited players in masks and socially distanced beginning in July 2020, just shy of four months since we last visited the facility. It was like a shot in the arm for many of the residents because they had not been allowed outside the care facilities, except for medical appointments—then placed in quarantine for a minimum of fourteen days. Thankfully, we have been allowed to perform our evangelistic music outreach every month since and throughout the pandemic. Each time it lifts the spirits of all, including the staff and nurses. Contagious joy and smiles abound. I hope to continue in this ministry as long as I see the benefits of it blessing both the participants and the recipients.

We have continued a hybrid rehearsal online via Zoom meeting and in-person with social distancing. Approximately a month ago, most of the players and residents completed their vaccinations, and this has started the gradual re-opening of the assisted living and memory care residents to visitors. We are looking forward to being back with them to cheer them on and remind them that they are not alone—God is with them, He loves them, and He will never fail or forsake them.

In conclusion, I would like to encourage church leaders to continue trusting the Lord for wisdom, guidance, and strength in their innovations to adapt methods and persevere in their efforts to share the Gospel message and make disciples. God has called us and will equip us. His resources are limitless. The joy of His presence is the best part of the journey. May we all keep our focus on Jesus and know that the task in front of us is never greater than the God who goes before us and is with us always. He will complete the good work He's started in and through us. We can rest assured that no labor in the Lord is ever in vain and look forward to His eternal reward for faithfulness in following Him.

About the Author

Rev. Dr. H. L. "Scooter" Ward, Jr. Scooter is the associate pastor and music minister of Community Church of Santa Rosa Beach located in northwest Florida. He also serves as President of the South Walton Ministry Association, a Kingdom-oriented, Christian cooperative of participating churches and parachurch organizations in Walton County, FL. He earned a B.A. in Theology from Southeastern Bible College in Birmingham, AL and received his commission as an officer in the United States Air Force where he served on active duty for nearly ten years as an Air Battle Manager on-board the E-3 Sentry (AWACS). A decorated combat veteran, Scooter also received an M.A. in Christian Studies & an M.Div. from Luther Rice Seminary in Lithonia, GA, and a Doctor of Worship Studies degree from the School of Music at Liberty University in Lynchburg, VA. Scooter and his wife, Amy, have been married for eighteen years and currently reside in Freeport, Florida. They both enjoy spending time with family, playing card games, swimming, and walking. When the opportunity presents itself, Scooter loves performing with his big band, Cloud 9 Orchestra, where he creatively shares the Gospel through music in patriotic and Christmas outreach events. He also leads two ukulele orchestras weekly at his church and they perform monthly as an outreach ministry to three local assisted living and memory care facilities.

COMMUNITY CHURCH OF SANTA ROSA BEACH
SANTA ROSA BEACH, FLORIDA

Year founded: 1940S
Denomination or Network: Nondenominational
Weekly Attendance: 130-180
Location: Suburban, 65 miles east of Pensacola
Website: srbcc.com

GREAT COMMISSION

RESEARCH JOURNAL

2021, Vol. 13(2) 105-107

Book Review

Microchurches: A Smaller Way

By Brian Sanders
Tampa, FL: Underground Media, 2019
132 pages
USD $14.99

Reviewed by: Jason L. Lalonde

Brian Sanders offers a stimulating, tilt-your-head experience in his book *Microchurches: A Smaller Way*, which seeks to champion the growing movement of a smaller church expression called "The Underground." Beyond possessing graduate degrees in Religious Studies from the University of South Florida and Applied Theology from Spurgeon's College, Sanders' acumen in writing on the validity and necessity of smaller churches comes from his experience in leading "The Underground" church network over the past two decades.

Microchurches is divided into two sections. Part One, "The Microchurch," explains microchurches to be the most basic, purest, and potent form of church and "is something that all of us can do" (10). Sanders makes his case in the first three chapters by appealing to our sensibilities in relationship to little children, our self-identification as a people who have been dispersed, and the power for kingdom impact arising from a collective embodiment of servanthood evangelism. Sanders concludes that when we look at children, it helps us to remember that "being small, simple, humble and pure, to come up short is merely to remind people exactly who they are" (12). When the church is scattered, it is able to diversify itself and go into spaces where other forms of church are not able to penetrate. And lastly, when the church organizes itself as a network of decentralized communities, it fosters a deep sense of ownership and a vibrant creativity in its mission to demonstrate the ways of Jesus in a particular context.

Chapters four through six flesh out the "minimal ecclesiology" of The Underground, which contains the three elements of worship, community and mission. It is important to note that a church affiliated with The Underground can add other essentials to be in their network, but it must maintain a commitment to worship, community and mission.

Part Two of *Microchurches* lays out the process for beginning a microchurch. It establishes the fact that planting a microchurch is open to anyone in chapter seven. Chapters eight through eleven set the sequence for execution. *Ideation* is the phase where you "have to articulate your ideas in order to form a team who will help influence and contribute" (71). From there you move to *iteration*, which is experimentation with the idea you've brought forth and where experiential learning is especially emphasized. Next, through experiencing successes and failures, you're able to "set some processes in place that are proven to work" (97), which is called *codification*. And then, after codification, comes *expansion* "which in the Kingdom of God implies an equilibrium between welcoming people in and sending people out" (107). Finally, chapter twelve ends the book by giving some practical guidance for those considering starting a microchurch out of their present church expression and highlights the importance of greater strength in networks.

The goal of Brian Sanders in *Microchurch* is to encourage the reader to consider, "What is necessary to be a church?" His conviction and practice at The Underground is that the bride of Christ most authentically expresses herself in the most basic practices of worship, community and mission by going small.

Beyond the strength of the minimal ecclesiology of The Underground, there is something to be said for the simplicity of the process in order to participate in the movement. The "four discernable overlapping and sometime recurring states" (63) of ideation, iteration, codification and expansion doesn't overwhelm the potential leader and group with massive details, administration and complexity. The simple rubric gives permission for creativity, experimentation, and failure, seeking to inspire the "What if…" residing in all of us.

Now, as for weaknesses in arguing for the microchurch throughout the book, I couldn't help but notice places of overstatement. For example, The Underground is immediately put forth as "a comprehensive alternative to the prevailing model of church in the West" (2). To call an expression of the church comprehensive in nature is bold, to say the least, and can unintentionally foster a "We are the right way" and an "us versus them" relationship with other kinds of churches.

Also, I found it sometimes distressing as to why Sanders seems to take such a hard line in suggesting that worship, community and mission can only take place in a smaller expression of the church. Wouldn't it be best to say these characteristics of the church need to be re-discovered in some churches, and then lay out the benefits? Is it possible The Underground is not merely a movement of going small, distinct and better than other expressions of the church, but is also offering a prophetic call to revitalization for the larger sized churches?

Overall, it is clear Sanders has a bias towards smaller groups and those who have "been disillusioned with or lost in the bigger expressions of church" (14), but that is also one of the reasons I enjoyed the book. With a growing population of religiously non-affiliated people in the West who are skeptical of large institutions, Sanders and The Underground are scratching an itch. This book however is not only for them but is also a challenge for all of God's people to truly rejoice in their worship, go deep in community and keep the gospel mission a priority.

GREAT COMMISSION
RESEARCH JOURNAL
2021, Vol. 13(2) 109-110

Book Review

The Culture Map: Breaking Through the Invisible Boundaries of Global Business

By Erin Meyer
New York, NY: PublicAffairs, 2014
288 pages
USD $28.00, Hardcover

Reviewed by Kenneth Nehrbass. Kenneth holds a Ph.D. in intercultural studies. He is an associate professor of Global Studies for the Rawlings School of Divinity at Liberty University.

Those who have been using the seminal theories within intercultural studies, such as Geert Hofstede's *Dimensions of Culture* and Edward Hall's *Silent Language,* will feel familiar with the eight dimensions in Meyer's *Culture Map.* Meyer's original contribution is that she has named each of the dyadic categories. She refers to the high/low context dyad as the "communication" dimension; the egalitarian/hierarchical dyad is the "leading" dimension; the task/relationship-based continuum is "trusting;" and flexible/loose time orientation is along a continuum called "scheduling." Meyer's other four dimensions are less discussed in the field of intercultural studies. They include evaluating, persuading, deciding, and disagreeing.

While much of this theory is introductory, albeit updated for the 21st century, and aimed specifically at the business world, Meyer does solve a few problems that have plagued the field of intercultural studies. First, critics claim the cultural domains discussed in the field of intercultural studies rely on essentialism. "Isn't it just a sophisticated form of stereotyping to say that Germans are blunt, and Italians are emotional, or that Americans are more punctual than Brazilians?" Meyer recognizes this weakness in intercultural studies; but she explains the differences between cultures are not like plots on a graph, contra Hofstede's *Dimension*—instead, there is overlapping distribution. Much of what an American encounters while working in a Japanese business context will feel familiar. At times though, an American will notice differences that can be readily explained by cultural tendencies such as the expected patterns for providing feedback or building trust.

Meyer digs deeper into these cultural domains than many other introductory texts. For example, interculturalists often indicate erroneously that English is a low context language whereas Japanese is high context. Meyer posits that language itself is neutral and is neither low nor high context. It is the *national culture* that impacts speakers' tolerance of ambiguity. English spoken in the US is very low context, whereas context is higher in the UK and even more contextual for English speakers in India.

Another way in which Meyer has pushed intercultural theory is her disaggregation of the concept of "direct/indirect speech." Americans, she notes, tend to be highly direct, but they beat around the bush when giving criticism. Israelis are the opposite. They tend to be proud of their ability to deliver indirect speech in many domains of life yet give their criticism directly. Overall, the recognition that a national culture's value orientation can vary *by domain* is a significant contribution to the field.

Meyer also innovatively deals with the question of whether there is such a thing as American culture. Much of the variation across the U.S. can be described by interpersonal, rather than cultural, differences. Americans are keenly aware that Southerners are quite different from New Englanders or Californians—until they go to New Delhi! Then they begin to think in terms of "Americans," as an aggregate, in contrast to South Asians. Meyer argues that much of the variation we encounter in the workplace is due to regional or interpersonal differences; nonetheless, national-level cultural preferences have helped tens of thousands of culture-crossers to understand their host culture and to adjust appropriately.

The text relies almost entirely on rich anecdotes to substantiate the eight dimensions. Unfortunately, Meyer seldom interacts with empirical research. Because of this methodological weakness, the text serves as an introduction to the concepts, but those who teach graduate courses in intercultural studies would also want to include qualitative or quantitative studies related to these domains.

2022 Great Commission Research Network Conference

Faith Sharing with Skeptics and Nones

March 7-8, 2022
Orlando, Florida

Call for Papers

This year's conference will be one of the Pre-Conferences at Exponential (Mar 8-10). Exponential, a large conference focused on church multiplication (exponential.org). The conference is held at First Baptist Church of Orlando. Information on hotels can be found on Exponential's website.

The price for both the Great Commission Research Network (GCRN) Conference and Exponential is $169. Please register at greatcommissionresearch.com/conference

The GCRN conference begins on Monday, March 7, at 1:00pm and ends Tuesday, March 8, at Noon, after which the Exponential conference begins and continues through Thursday.

If you are interested in presenting research, please email a 100-200 word summary of your proposed presentation to Jay Moon, President of the GCRN, at jay.moon@asburyseminary.edu. Proposals will be accepted based on quality of research, relevance to the theme of the conference, and potential for application in local churches.

CALL FOR PAPERS

Knox Fellowship Awards 2022
RESEARCH IN EVANGELISM
Sponsored by the Great Commission Research Network and Knox Fellowship

Purpose:
The Great Commission Research Network and Knox Fellowship are sponsoring the 2022 Call for Papers and awards for Research in Evangelism, with winning and outstanding papers to be considered for publication in the Fall 2022 issue of the *Great Commission Research Journal*. The goal of the competition is to compile and disseminate research that serves to help churches fulfill the Great Commission (Matt. 28:18-20).

Submissions (Due April 30):
Papers should present original research not yet published relevant to the field of evangelism. They should be 3000-7000 words and in APA format. Submissions should be emailed by May 15, 2022, to David Dunaetz, editor of the *Great Commission Research Journal*: ddunaetz@apu.edu

Publication and Awards:
Four $500 awards will be granted to papers in any of the following categories. **Students are especially encouraged to submit papers.**

1) **Theological Research**
   -Focusing on developing a biblical theology of some theme relevant to contemporary evangelism.
2) **Empirical Research**
   -Reporting quantitative research (e.g., hypothesis testing with survey data) or qualitative research (e.g., interviews to answer a research question) on a topic relevant to evangelism.
3) **Case Studies**
   -A description and analysis of evangelism in a specific context (e.g., a local church).

The most valuable contributions will be considered for publication in the Fall 2022 issue of the *Great Commission Research Journal*. If there are a sufficient number of valuable contributions, they may be published in a book.

GREAT COMMISSION RESEARCH NETWORK

(formerly: The American Society for Church Growth)

OFFICERS

President:
Dr. Jay Moon
Professor of Church Planting and Evangelism
Asbury Theological Seminary
Email: jay.moon@asburyseminary.edu

First Vice President:
Dr. Brad Ransom
Chief Training Officer
Director of Church Planting
Free Will Baptist North American Ministries
Email: brad@nafwb.org

Treasurer:
Ben Penfold
Chief Executive Officer
Penfold & Company

GREAT COMMISSION RESEARCH NETWORK
greatcommissionresearch.com

MEMBERSHIP

What is the Great Commission Research Network?

The Great Commission Research Network (GCRN) is a worldwide and professional association of Christian leaders whose ministry activities have been influenced by the basic and key principles of church growth as originally developed by the late Donald McGavran. Founded by renowned missiologists George G. Hunter III and C. Peter Wagner, the GCRN has expanded into an affiliation of church leaders who share research, examine case studies, dialogue with cutting-edge leaders, and network with fellow church professionals who are committed to helping local churches expand the kingdom through disciple-making.

Who Can Join the GCRN?

GCRN membership is open to all who wish a professional affiliation with colleagues in the field. The membership includes theoreticians, such as professors of evangelism and missions, and practitioners, such as pastors, denominational executives, parachurch leaders, church planters, researchers, mission leaders, and consultants. Some members specialize in domestic or mono-cultural church growth, while others are cross-culturally oriented.

Why Join the GCRN?

The GCRN provides a forum for maximum interaction among leaders, ministries, and resources on the cutting edge of Great Commission research. The annual conference of the GCRN (typically held in March each year) offers the opportunity for research updates and information on new resources and developments, as well as fellowship and encouragement from colleagues in the field of church growth. Membership in the GCRN includes a subscription to the *Great Commission Research Journal* and a discount for the annual conference.

How Do I Join the GCRN?

For further information on membership and the annual conference, please visit greatcommissionresearch.com.

Membership Fees

- One-year regular membership (inside or outside USA) - $59
- One-year student/senior adult membership (inside or outside USA) - $39
- Three-year regular membership (inside or outside USA) - $177
- Three-year senior membership (inside or outside USA) - $117
- Membership includes a subscription to the *Great Commission Research Journal* which is in the process of transitioning to an electronic format.

GREAT COMMISSION RESEARCH NETWORK
AWARDS

Donald A. McGavran Award for Outstanding Leadership in Great Commission Research

Normally once each year, the GCRN gives this award to an individual for exemplary scholarship, intellect, and leadership in the research and dissemination of the principles of effective disciple-making as described by Donald A. McGavran. The award recipients to date:

Win Arn	1989	Rick Warren	2004
C. Peter Wagner	1990	Charles Arn	2005
Carl F. George	1991	John Vaughan	2006
Wilbert S. McKinley	1992	Waldo Werning	2006
Robert Logan	1993	Bob Whitesel	2007
Bill Sullivan	1994	Bill Easum	2009
Elmer Towns	1994	Thom S. Rainer	2010
Flavil R. Yeakley Jr.	1995	Ed Stetzer	2012
George G. Hunter III	1996	Nelson Searcy	2013
Eddie Gibbs	1997	J. D. Payne	2014
Gary L. McIntosh	1998	Alan McMahan	2015
Kent R. Hunter	1999	Steve Wilkes	2016
R. Daniel Reeves	2000	Art McPhee	2016
Ray Ellis	2002	Mike Morris	2017
John Ellas	2003	Bill Day	2019

Win Arn Lifetime Achievement Award in Great Commission Research

This award is given to a person who has excelled in the field of American church growth over a long period of time. The award recipients to date:

Eddie Gibbs	2011	Gary McIntosh	2015
Elmer Towns	2012	Kent R. Hunter	2017
George G. Hunter III	2013	Carl George	2019
John Vaughan	2014		

American Society for Church Growth/GCRN Past Presidents

C. Peter Wagner	1986	Ray W. Ellis	1999-00
George G. Hunter III	1987	Charles Van Engen	2001-02
Kent R. Hunter	1988	Charles Arn	2003-04
Elmer Towns	1989	Alan McMahan	2005-06
Eddie Gibbs	1990	Eric Baumgartner	2007-08
Bill Sullivan	1991	Bob Whitesel	2009-12
Carl F. George	1992	Steve Wilkes	2013-14
Flavil Yeakley Jr.	1993	Mike Morris	2015-16
John Vaughan	1994	James Cho	2017-18
Gary L. McIntosh	1995-96	Gordon Penfold	2019-20
R. Daniel Reeves	1997-98		

GREAT COMMISSION RESEARCH NETWORK

SUBMISSIONS

The *Great Commission Research Journal* publishes both peer-reviewed articles reporting original research and reviews of recent books relevant to evangelism and disciple making.

The scope of the journal includes research focusing on evangelism, church planting, church growth, spiritual formation, church renewal, worship, or missions. Articles come from both members and non-members of the Great Commission Research Network and are generally unsolicited submissions, which are welcomed and will be considered for peer-review. There is no charge for submission or publication.

ARTICLES

All submissions should be emailed to the editor, David R. Dunaetz at ddunaetz@apu.edu.

Peer Review Process

Only the highest quality submissions presenting original research within the scope of the journal will be chosen for publication. To ensure this, all articles will go through a peer review process. Articles deemed by the editor to have potential for publication will be sent to reviewers (members of the editorial board or other reviewers with the needed expertise) for their recommendation. Upon receiving the reviewers' recommendations, the author will be notified that the submission was either rejected, that the submission has potential but needs to be significantly revised and resubmitted, that the submission is conditionally accepted if the noted issues are addressed, or that the submission is accepted unconditionally.

Format

Papers should be APA formatted according to the 7th edition of the Publication Manual of the American Psychological Association. Submissions should include a cover page, be double-spaced in Times New Roman, and be between 3,000 and 7,000 words (approximately 10-22 pages) in .docx format. Contact the editor for exceptions to this word count.

In-text references should be in the form (Smith, 2020) or (Smith, 2020, p.100). At the end of the article should be a References section. No footnotes should be used. Minimize the use of endnotes. If endnotes are necessary, more than two or three are strongly discouraged; rather than using Microsoft Word's endnote tool, place them manually before the References section.

Include an abstract of approximately 100-150 words at the beginning of your text.

After the References section, include a short biography (approximately 30 words) for each author.

BOOK REVIEWS

The purpose of our book reviews is to direct the reader to books that contribute to the broader disciple making endeavors of the church. The review (500-2000 words) is to help potential readers understand how the book will contribute to their ministry, especially those in North America or which have a large cross-cultural base. The review should consist of a summary of the contents, an evaluation of the book, and a description of how the book is applicable to practitioners.

Before submitting a book review, please contact the book review editor Dr. Kelton Hinton (khinton247@gmail.com) to either propose a book to be reviewed or to ask if there is a book that needs to be reviewed.

COPYRIGHT

CONTACT INFORMATION

To submit an article or for general questions, contact:
Dr. David Dunaetz, ddunaetz@apu.edu

For questions about book reviews, contact:
Dr. Kelton Hinton, khinton247@gmail.com